Feeding on Infinity

Feeding on Infinity

Readings in the Romantic Rhetoric of Internalization

Joshua Wilner

The Johns Hopkins University Press

BALTIMORE AND LONDON

© 2000 The Johns Hopkins University Press
All rights reserved. Published 2000
Printed in the United States of America on acid-free paper
9 8 7 6 5 4 3 2 1

The Johns Hopkins University Press
2715 North Charles Street
Baltimore, Maryland 21218-4363
www.press.jhu.edu

Library of Congress Cataloging-in-Publication Data will be found at the end of this book.
A catalog record for this book is available from the British Library.
ISBN 0-8018-6324-4

For Neil Hertz

A meditation rose in me that night
Upon the lonely mountain when the scene
Had passed away, and it appeared to me
The perfect image of a mighty mind,
Of one that feeds upon infinity . . .

WORDSWORTH,
The Prelude (1805)

Im Haschisch sind wir geniessende Prosawesen
höchster Potenz.

BENJAMIN,
"Haschisch in Marseilles" (1932)

Contents

Acknowledgments

*W*orking on this book has kept me out of worse mischief for many years, and accordingly there are many—from family and friends to students, teachers, and colleagues—who may owe it a nod of thanks. For myself, I find it impossible to properly acknowledge my many and varied debts to those who stood by me in body and spirit during its writing. I do wish to communicate a particular word of thanks to Cynthia Chase for responding to the manuscript with the generosity, attentiveness, and critical insight that are hers.

An earlier version of chapter 2 appears in *Midrash and Literature,* ed. Geoffrey H. Hartman and Sanford Budick (Yale University Press, 1986). Permission to reprint is gratefully acknowledged. Earlier versions of chapters 6 and 7 appear in *MLN* 104 (1989): 5 and *Diacritics* 27 (1997): 3, respectively. Work on the project was supported in part by a grant from the Simon H. Rifkind Center for the Humanities and the Arts at CCNY and by a PSC-CUNY Creative Incentive Award.

Note on Editions and Translations

*U*nless otherwise noted, all citations from works by Baudelaire, Rousseau, and Montaigne are referenced to the Pléiade editions; all citations from Wordsworth's *Prelude* are from the 1805 version as printed in the Norton Critical Edition; all citations from works by Nietzsche are referenced to the three-volume Schlecta edition; all citations from works by Freud are referenced to the multivolume Standard Edition.

All translations given in brackets are my own except where credited to another source.

Feeding on Infinity

One

Interface

*T*he essays gathered here concern the problem of internalization as it finds expression in the European Romantic literary
tradition. They pursue this inquiry from various angles, but always by examining specific texts.

When Wordsworth reflects on the scene he beholds from the slopes of
Snowdon as the emblem of a mind "that feeds upon infinity," we sense that
it is above all the figure of "feeding" that is doing the work. But can we say
what work it is doing? Can we say what this turn of phrase has to do with the
poet's recurrence in memory to those "spots of time" by which "our minds
are nourished and invisibly repaired" as a fund of imaginative power, or with
his blessing of the nursing babe "who gather[s]" (in a later version "drinks
in") "passion from his mother's eye"? Looking forward, do we know the history (Is there a history?) that leads from Wordsworth's poetic words of recognition and praise to Benjamin's more cramped and cryptic assessment that
"in hashish we are savoring prose beings to the highest power" ("im
Haschisch sind wir geniessende Prosawesen höchster Potenz" [*Illuminationen,* 349])? The wager in all these essays is that such formulations and the reflections they condense involve deeply embedded if obscure registrations of
early and ongoing transactions between an imperfectly constituted self and
its objects; that these dealings inform the critical and creative power of poetic language generally; and collaterally, that Romanticism's increasing explicitation of these interactions participates in the long and continuing story
of patriarchy's decline in the West.

Not too long ago, the late Raymond Carver grouped a collection of stories under the title of one, "What We Talk about When We Talk about Love,"
and in a more academic and comic vein I have toyed with the idea of calling
this collection "What *Do* We Talk about When We Talk about Internaliza-

tion?" For such talk is surprisingly common, crossing the boundaries of literary studies, psychoanalysis, and ideological critique and passing into everyday use,[1] but the processes and concepts we thus tag are not by the same token well grasped, if grasped at all. Accordingly, these readings pursue a labor of conceptual clarification (what Wittgenstein might call a grammatical investigation were the language practices under consideration less specialized or less inwrought with rhetorical complication) at least as much as they extend the application of provisionally secured concepts to fresh material. And this is less a function of the relative newness of the discourse (a discourse that, after all, has a history reaching well back into the nineteenth century if one considers its antecedents in Hegel)[2] than of the constitutive resistance of the phenomena under consideration to conceptual tools that, however serviceable and gratifying to manipulate in certain contexts, here lack a steady point of application.

Chapter 2 ("Romanticism and the Internalization of Scripture") examines in detail some of the difficulties surrounding the use of internalization as a category of literary-historical and rhetorical analysis, a matter I will comment on briefly later in this introduction. I have chosen to initiate this book, however, with some remarks on the *psychoanalytic* problem of internalization, for two related reasons. First of all, this is an area many readers are likely to already be somewhat familiar with, given the immense influence of Freud's account of superego formation, the principal context within which his theory of internalization was elaborated. Second, although I did not in fact begin investigating the problem of internalization in literary studies from a psychoanalytic perspective, I have increasingly found it to be an area where the two fields are joined at the hip—much too closely for either one's comfort. In starting out, then, from the relatively familiar terrain of psychoanalysis, I hope to move more quickly toward this troublesome interface than I could by approaching it via the more densely mediated discourses of literary theory.[3]

In contemporary psychoanalytic parlance it is customary to distinguish between "primary" and "secondary" internalization, on the model of Freud's distinction between primary and secondary narcissism. The latter has to do with transactions that go on between an already differentiated psyche and significant objects and functions in its environment, whereas the former concerns processes by which the most rudimentary psychic divisions between what is me and what is not me, what is "inner" and what is "outer," get established in the first place. About secondary internalization, particularly superego formation, psychoanalysis has much to say, but about primary internalization it says relatively little. Thus, for example, W. W. Meissner remarks at the outset of *Internalization in Psychoanalysis*, a lucid work of distillation and synthesis to which I am much indebted: "For the most part we shall be dealing with secondary internalization and externalization. The primary forms of internalization and externalization occur in the earliest stages of psychic development and their basic nature remains obscure" (11).

What remains obscure within the psychoanalytic discussion of internalization (and, complementarily, externalization) is in Meissner's own terms not a subsidiary matter but rather something "basic" and "primary." At the same time, his formulation implies something about the reasons for this abiding obscurity: for to speak of "the earliest stages of psychic development" is to dimly conjure with words processes that lie on the far side of language, but perhaps *just* on the far side and eventuating in its acquisition and consolidation. The difficulty psychoanalysis experiences in trying to speak clearly about "the primary forms of internalization and externalization," and that contrasts with its prolific discourse on their "secondary" forms, would thus, at least structurally, be related to the infant's early efforts to express itself through speech.[4]

Working from a developmental perspective, Meissner presents this zone of obscurity as residing within the domain of primary internalization, and thus as receding in importance as one turns one's attention to secondary internalization. This book differs in proposing that the operations of internalization always involve crossing a linguistic threshold and that the representational issues that attend this crossing cannot be consigned to an early stage within a progressive development. For when examined closely, the term "internalization" displays another bifurcation somewhat different from the developmental distinction between primary and secondary internalization that Meissner refers to. On the one hand, it refers to the inhibition and involution of energies arising from within and tending toward outward discharge. (As such it may be applied to ideas of both inhibited action and inhibited utterance—and since an utterance may already be the derivative of an internalized impulse, the inhibited utterance may involve a compounded "internalization." This latter relation is explored further in chapter 5, "Action, Internalization, and Utterance: Structure and Gender in the Romantic Lyric.") On the other hand, "internalization" refers to the literal, metaphorical, or phantasmatic transfer of some entity and its associated functions from an "outside" to an "inside." In this sense, for example, "the internalization of language" designates something quite other than a modality of inhibition.

As I discuss at greater length in the first part of chapter 3 ("Monster Feedback: Retrospection, Traumatic Internalization, and Perceptual Aberration in *Prelude* 1"), these two dimensions of meaning are always mutually implicated in Freud's writings about internalization, even if at times one is more foregrounded than the other. Thus, to cite an example that is neither simply one example among others nor an immovable reigning paradigm, in Freud's account of superego formation the superego is compounded *both* of aggressive impulses turned back on the self and of features derived from a parental model.

Furthermore, the articulation of these two aspects of internalization is *contingent* with regard to the passions and objects it binds. That is to say, it depends for its occurrence on a constellation of circumstances whose elements are variable, though they may have typical instantiations (as in Freud's account). Nor is this contingent articulation simply a matter of association, if by association we mean contiguity in space and time. Rather, its nearest model is linguistic: it is like the verbal relay connecting semantic fields and grammatical functions that may otherwise be discontinuous. As such, it is a form of articulation that disrupts the homogeneity of any particular spatiotemporal field of representation. In this conceptualization, then, processes of internalization involve a moment that is in fact alien to inner/outer dichotomies and the forms of intelligibility they underwrite. And what we call "internalization" paradoxically entails the self-occluding imposition of a spatial figure on a quasi-linguistic phenomenon. From this perspective, the area of obscurity Meissner's account acknowledges needs to be understood not only genetically, as the shadowy trace of early psychological processes, but also structurally in terms of the disruptive relation of language to spatial and temporal ordering. Psychoanalysis can elaborate a theoretically continuous account of secondary internalization only to the extent that it remains haunted by this disruptive linguistic element.[5]

Thus far I have sought to illustrate with a few broad strokes why and where the psychoanalytic theory of internalization may become of interest to the theory and practice of literary reading. But the question remains why the investigation of such rudimentary and presumably transhistorical structures and processes should be *especially* relevant to the study of a historically restricted set of largely canonical literary artifacts. Or to turn the question around, Why bring the reading of a few European Romantic and post-Romantic texts to bear on an understanding of the problem of internalization? One aspiration of these essays, taken collectively, is to demonstrate in practice the richness and complexity of the field of inquiry thus opened. But some programmatic words of explanation, backed by the consideration of some paradigmatic examples, may be in order here at the outset.

First of all, and as I discuss at greater length in chapter 2, although defining Romanticism is a standing problem for literary history, some notion of internalization at the level of cultural tradition has recurrently been proposed as the *solution* to that problem. To take a relatively recent and forthright example, consider the title of Harold Bloom's influential "The Internalization of Quest-Romance" (1970), from which the basic thesis of the essay may readily be inferred: "The poet takes the patterns of quest-romance and transposes them into his own imaginative life" (5).[6] Whether Bloom would care to stand by this characterization of Romanticism now I cannot say, but in any case it represents an inventive, concise, and compelling variation on a familiar literary-historical theme.

The very simplicity of the schema of course invites skepticism, and "the interpretation of Romanticism as interiorization" in Paul de Man's equally concise, but now polemical, characterization (*Aesthetic Ideology*, 190n) has not wanted for critics. But in this debate the notion of internalization tends to be handled on both sides as a known quantity, whereas I am arguing that the notion itself remains obscure and thus that the *problem* of internalization and the *problem* of Romanticism may indeed, with respect to the discourse of literary history, be closely intertwined.[7]

Second, and perhaps more interesting, contemporary discussions of internalization, whether their primary concern is with psychic, literary, or ideological patterns of formation, tend to derive in more or less mediated fashion from the theoretical practice of writers of the Romantic period, understood in its restricted historical sense.[8] It is an easy matter, for example, to connect Freud on *Verinnerlichung* [internalization] to Nietzsche on the same subject, and thence to Nietzsche's various forerunners in post-Kantian German Romantic culture.[9] And though Wordsworth's complex relation to eighteenth-century associationist psychology is well known, that psychology acquires a surprisingly anticipatory resonance in Wordsworthian formulations such as this footnote from the 1815 Preface: "Guided by one of my own primary consciousnesses, I have represented a commutation and transfer of internal feelings, cooperating with external accidents, to plant, for immortality, images of sound and sight, in the celestial soil of the Imagination" (*Selected Poems and Prefaces*, 487n). Similarly, though nothing like the term "internalization" forms part of Rousseau's critical vocabulary, his critique of Hobbes and other state of nature political theorists in *The Second Discourse* for having "transporté à l'état de Nature, des idées qu'ils avoient prises dans la société" [carried over to the state of nature ideas acquired in society] (*Oeuvres complètes,* 3:132) establishes the link, now so familiar as to be taken for granted, between the intimate internalization of social norms and ideological mystification.[10] Thus, to investigate internalization by reading Romantic texts is to return to a point at which that problem is first being taken hold of as such, the soil still clinging to its roots.

If this latter claim is correct, it leads to a consideration of why the syntax and vocabulary that allow for the investigation of this field of understanding should have begun to develop at this particular time. Although the historical dimension of the current project is based on too narrow a sampling of material to claim other than speculative value, I argue that the development and transformation of the discursive practices in question are bound up with the history of patriarchy in the West, with the ambiguous role that male Romantic writers played in the reproduction of patriarchal cultural authority, and with the breakdown, clearly heralded by Wordsworth's "Preface to *Lyrical Ballads,*" of the foundational generic distinction between the language of poetry and the language of prose, an organizing principle that had become closely intertwined with gender hierarchies. In my reading of this history, pre-Oedipal patterns of incorporation and the primary but highly unstable processes of subject and symbol formation they underwrite become increasingly salient as the unacknowledged—and a fortiori uninterrogated—dominance of classically Oedipal patterns of cultural transmission and the mechanisms of internalization associated with them become sufficiently weakened to be open to questioning.[11] The emergence with psychoanalysis of an explicit theory of internalization, for which Romanticism lays the groundwork, is itself symptomatic of this development (even as that theory retains a weakened prescriptive force), as is the subsequent emergence within the history of psychoanalysis of object-relations theory.

THUS FAR I have been talking in general terms about patterns of internalization that gain salience in Romantic writing and noting some critical approaches to their analysis. I now turn to an inaugural moment in this history, both to bring into sharper focus the patterns under consideration and to accentuate the particular historical cast of the chapters that follow. I take as my proof text the opening paragraphs, sometimes referred to as the preamble, of Rousseau's *Confessions,* which I consider in relation to the notice "Au lecteur" that Montaigne had placed between the title page and the body of his *Essais* two centuries before. (These prefatory texts are cited in their entirety, with translations, in appendixes A and B.)

The two openings have often been compared, and with good reason: Montaigne's sly self-deprecation and Rousseau's unabashed "profession de soi" are rhetorical mirror images, correspondingly ironic and hyperbolic studies in the act of publicly, but from the place of the work itself, averring the singular truthfulness of the writer's self-representation. One could also point to numerous points of verbal contact between the two passages, and unpublished draft material dispels any doubt that Rousseau had Montaigne's notice to the reader closely in mind in writing his own.[12] Indeed, it is difficult for the reader familiar with Montaigne—as, of course, Rousseau's initial readership would have been—to move beyond the opening sentences of the preamble without recognizing that Rousseau's self-figuration as truth teller is produced via the negation and transformative incorporation of Montaigne's claims.[13]

For our purposes, however, both the similarities and the differences of the two passages are centered in a slight but highly overdetermined figural shift. Specifically, Montaigne identifies truthful self-representation with the exhibition of one's body in its nakedness:

> Mes defauts s'y liront au vif, et ma forme naïfve, autant que la reverence publique me l'a permis. Que si j'eusse esté entre ces nations qu'on dict vivre encore sous la douce liberté des premieres loix de nature, je t'asseure que je m'y fusse très-volontiers peint tout entier, et tout nud.
>
> [My faults will show through vividly, and my native form, insofar as respect for the public has permitted. For were I among those nations that are said to still live under the sweet liberty of nature's first laws, I assure you that I would have readily painted myself in the altogether and quite naked.][14]

But Rousseau writes of unveiling not the body's vulnerable surface, but its interior:

> J'ai dévoilé mon intérieur tel que tu l'as vu toi-même. Être etérnel . . .
>
> [I have unveiled my interior as you yourself have seen it. Eternal Being . . .]

Although this difference in figuration may seem trivial or simply the substitution of one rhetorical commonplace for another, I would argue that it is the index of a far-ranging transformation of the cultural work the act of self-representation is being called on to perform, a transformation that enters deeply, even violently, into the structure and experience of the self-representing subject. (A century later, Baudelaire would render graphic both the banality and the phantasmatic violence of this figural shift with his working title for an intimate journal, "Mon coeur mis à nu" [My heart laid bare].)

Why speak of this inward turn as overdetermined? First of all, as already noted, Rousseau's assertions of veracity depend for their articulation on a negation of Montaigne's claims: the self is situated in a closed circuit of self-affection and self-cognition, but the purity of this space can be constituted only through an expulsion of the other, which has to be occluded if it is to perform its function. But beyond this familiar dialectic of self-reference, Rousseau's figure of inwardness also functions as an intensification of Montaigne's location of the writer's body as the figural center of attention. For the figure of the unveiled interior repeats as it inverts the body's relation to the surrounding world, from which it is differentiated but on which it depends for its existence, and makes of the body's surface a Janus-like entity, one side turned inward and in communication with the encrypted self, the other turned outward toward the world.[15]

It is not, then, that Rousseau's picturing of the true self as inner is in itself novel; on the contrary, that picture is part and parcel of the eschatological tradition whose imagery he explicitly invokes (and Montaigne implicitly forgoes). What is new, and gives the contrast with Montaigne its historical specificity, is Rousseau's conflation of an apocalyptic tableau with a rhetorical spectacle whose antecedents are more classical and political than Christian and religious. Thus, although Rousseau envisions presenting himself, book in hand, on Judgment Day at the throne of "the Eternal Being," it is not to that Being, who has already seen into Rousseau's interior, that his confessions are ultimately addressed, but to the assembled multitude of his fellows. The function of the "sovereign judge" is reduced to that of a transcendental witness who may vouch for the truthfulness of Rousseau's testimony before the jury of his peers. This appeal to a transcendental witness is of a piece with the impossibility of any other human being's performing this role. Indeed, it is precisely because the truth of Rousseau's being is known to none but himself that he must publish his *Confessions*, lest the disfiguring image of him in public circulation prevail and posterity fail to make a just assessment of his worth.[16]

In striking contrast, Montaigne presents himself as writing his book only for those who already know him:

Je l'ay voué à la commodité particuliere de mes parens et amis: à ce que m'ayant perdu (ce qu'ils ont à faire bien tost) ils y puissent retrouver aucuns traits de mes conditions et humeurs, et que par ce moyen ils nourrisent plus entiere et plus vifve la connoissance qu'ils ont eu de moy.

[I have intended it for the particular use of my family and friends, so that having lost me (as soon they will), they may find in it some traces of my ways and dispositions and so nourish more completely and more vividly their recollection of me.]

This claim, of course, cannot be taken at face value, because it functions as a lure to imagine oneself a member of that intimate circle, and because the characteristic and uncanny effect of Montaigne's writing is indeed to produce in every reader precisely the anamnetic effect of recognition he speaks about. Moreover, no less than Rousseau's writing, though according to a different modality, it puts into play a trope of interiorization when he speaks of his readers' "nourishing" through reading (and here we may recall Wordsworth's "nourishing" spots of time) their recollection of him, and its deployment of this trope is inseparable from Montaigne's patriarchal position among the family and friends whose circle he conjures and whom he casts as the proper recipients of his legacy. It is in part the security of this social position that enables Montaigne to acknowledge in a positive form the mediating role of the other—of the reader—in the constitution and transmission of his identity. If in this last regard he seems closer to us than Rousseau does, it must also be said that it is in part because Rousseau is in no position to inherit that social role that he seeks to ground his identity in more metaphysical fashion and by appeal to a more hyperbolic interiority.

IN TAKING Rousseau's preamble as an inaugural moment in the cultural history this book is concerned with, I have concentrated on its transformations of a certain topography of self-representation. But the problem of internalization in Romantic writing also presents itself in the salient use of figures of bodily incorporation—in particular metaphors and metonyms of eating and drinking—to represent and enact these transformations. Since I am as concerned with the strong physicality of these figures as with the more schematic transformations they condense, I conclude this introduction by turning to the signal instance from which I draw my title.

In the closing book of *The Prelude,* after the scene beheld from Snowdon has faded, Wordsworth reflects on what he has seen and heard:

> A meditation rose in me that night,
> Upon the lonely mountain when the scene
> Had passed away, and it appeared to me
> The perfect image of a mighty mind,
> Of one that feeds upon infinity,
> That is exalted by an under-presence,
> The sense of God, or whatsoe'er is dim
> Or vast in its own being . . .   (13.66–73)

With these lines, Wordsworth begins to slip from the recollection of an *earlier* meditation into the current of reflection that carries *The Prelude* to its close, a shift that is initiated with the use of a generalized present tense in the phrase "one that feeds upon infinity." The verb "feeds" thus relays the flow from past rumination to present declaration and does so via a discreet verbal equivocation that weakens the ordering power of logicotemporal patterns of subordination and sequence. At the same time that the present-tense verb "feeds" functions in this way, it *figures* a relation of contact and transfer between a finite mind ("one") and something that exceeds containment (infinity) yet through contact with which the mind is not only sustained but "exalted." Thus the word also opaquely figures the articulating function it performs by virtue of its grammatical indeterminacy.

I have already proposed that the terms in which Wordsworth describes those "spots of time" by which "our minds / Are nourished and invisibly repaired" (11.264–65) lead us to the same imaginative region as Snowdon's evocation of a "mind . . . [which] feeds upon infinity." The former passage also makes explicit the crucial, but surprisingly complicated, link between memory and internalization in Wordsworth. That the figure of "spots of time" both is radically condensed and names a locus of symbolic condensation is obvious enough, but the conjoined figure of the mind drawing nourishment at these spots is usually passed over, no doubt as a mere instance of garden variety Romantic organicism. Yet what seems like a casual enough word choice (for which one might substitute, for example, "strengthened") turns out to be intimately connected with the process of figuration by which the memory traces of certain experiences associated with different places are themselves pictured as places within an inner space. Thus, for example, in

Wordsworth's apostrophe to the Wye in "Tintern Abbey" ("How oft in spirit have I turned to thee!"), the apostrophic turn to the river as object of address is implicitly identified with the prior, recurrent turn "in spirit" it invokes, where the phrase "in spirit" encompasses the internalized character of both the silent appeal and the remembered place. Such "spots" (in a manner not unrelated to the way the figure of "mon intérieur" in Rousseau's preamble identifies the space of self-affection with the object of a transcendental gaze) both concentrate a space of interiority and mark within it—like so many periods, so many spots of ink[17]—the traces of a process of inscription. As we will see clearly in looking at the boat-stealing episode of *Prelude* 1, the event that thus leaves its trace within bodily memory is inseparable from its boundary crossing deposition (in the radical sense in which the event, figured as site, detaches itself from the particular time and place of an initial occurrence).

At the same time, the configuration of the Snowdon landscape as a whole invites comparison with the "Blessed Babe" tableau (2.237–80). The similarity in Wordsworth's descriptions of the power of the imagination as exemplified in the landscape and the activity of the infant mind, "our first poetic spirit," has been noted by commentators (e.g., the Norton *Prelude* editors, 462n), but a more graphic superimposition of the two scenes suggests itself as well. Specifically, the oblique gaze passing between the mother's eye and the child evokes the line of force that connects the moon to the breach in the mist, while this breach also, as a "breathing place" that draws down to "the voice of waters" rising through the mist, seems to have some disturbed relation to the mouth of "the babe, / Nursed in his mother's arms, the babe who sleeps / Upon his mother's breast."[18]

The possibility of thus superimposing the blessed babe tableau like a Cimabue Madonna on the Snowdon nightscape and of connecting both these scenes with the "spots of time" passage is in itself evidence of the degree of imaginative investment bound up in their convergent figures of feeding. Let us now return directly to the Snowdon passage to see whether we can offer a preliminary answer to the question this chapter set out from: Can we say what *work* the figure of "feeding" is doing in these lines? We have seen how in each passage the figure marks a peculiar interface that is also a point of discontinuity within a movement toward integration—between the infant's gazing eye and nursing mouth, between the future of poetic address and the past of recollection, between the remote and naked glory of the moon and the near but veiled roaring of the "real" sea. And we can now see how each of these configurations involves the articulation of a structure of reflection with one of transfer not unlike the bifurcated structure we detected earlier in the psychoanalytic "model" of internalization.

*   *   *

ALTHOUGH most of the chapters that follow originated as essays written for particular occasions, in bringing them together I have tried to shape a whole that would amount to more than the sum of its parts. The first, "Romanticism and the Internalization of Scripture," is also the most purely theoretical and programmatic, expanding on a number of theses, particularly with respect to the historiography of Romanticism, here more asserted than argued. The next two essays, "Monster Feedback" and "The Autobiographical Object," are decidedly more exegetical in emphasis and begin the work of probing the interface between rhetorical and psychoanalytic concepts of internalization. The two that follow, "Action, Internalization, and Utterance" and "The Stewed Muse of Prose," continue this exploration while considering the ways later writing begins to desublimate the patterns of internalization at work in "high" Romantic literature, and especially poetry, and in the process disturb the related hierarchies of gender and genre with which the sublimation of those patterns was allied. These are followed in turn by two chapters, "Drinking Rules!" and "Le Bonheur Vomitif," that examine more directly the relation between a certain modern conception of the "prosaic" and the explicitation of patterns of incorporation that we glimpse briefly in the sentences from Montagine. The last brief piece comparing two autobiographical narratives about spanking (one drawn from the first book of Rousseau's *Confessions,* the other from Eve Kosofsky Sedgwick's autobiographical weaving of prose and poetry titled "A Poem Is Being Written") is offered by way of measuring something of the distance traveled while at the same time suggesting that the difficult history traced in the preceding essays is by no means a "thing of the past" but continues to be played out in (Or should that be on?) our "post(int)eriority."

Two

Romanticism and the Internalization of Scripture

*A*s is well known, the intensity of critical debate in recent years surrounding the advent of "theory" has derived in significant measure from an open questioning of the received distinction between literature and its interpretation. One encounters in a variety of guises a growing interest in the imaginative dimension of exegesis: the freedom of its elaborations, the figurative texture of its own language, its narrative modulations. Yet there is a renewed insistence on the exegetic power of literary texts: the ways they "read" other texts, the ways they explicate themselves, the ways they thematize and sustain reflection on questions of hermeneutic theory.

Why this unsettling of the relation between text and interpretation has enjoyed and continues to enjoy an institutional sanction is a complex historical question. Certainly the situation can be traced in part to tensions latent in the new criticism's emphasis on close reading and the autonomous authority of the literary text, and to analogous tensions on the Continent that emerged with the development of structuralist poetics.[1] But this partial explanation obviously leads quickly to more fundamental questions. What are the conditions under which secular literary texts become candidates for the kind of demanding interpretative attention more commonly reserved for sacred texts, and what are the differences between the kinds of authority ascribed to literature and to Scripture?

One habitual answer to these questions among literary historians is that literature increasingly assumes autonomous cultural authority in the West as the authority of sacred texts comes into question. A crisis in this transition is usually situated sometime in the late eighteenth and early nineteenth centuries and is often defined in terms of a historical dialectic in which Romanticism is the synthesis or outcome of a conflict between belief in the authority of a scriptural tradition and scientific rationalism (or more generally, "materialism" in the varying meanings of that term). Literature in this view, like religion, would involve the intrusion into thought and social life of a radical otherness, and the tendency to read more intrinsically would be seen as a response to this radical autonomy. At the same time, the status of the literary text is to be construed in opposition to that of the sacred text, since it apparently abjures both ethical and epistemological claims, retaining only a reflexive and aesthetic authority—its knowledge of itself as fiction and as figure rather than as positive truth.

M. H. Abrams's encyclopedic and highly influential *Natural Supernaturalism,* which develops and documents an account of Romanticism as a "displaced and reconstituted theology" (65), may be cited here as representative. In his preface, Abrams summarizes this view:

> It is a historical commonplace that the course of Western thought since the Renaissance has been one of progressive secularization, but it is easy to mistake the way in which the process took place. Secular thinkers have no more been able to work free of the centuries old Judeo-Christian culture than Christian theologians were able to work free of their inheritance of classical and pagan thought. The process— outside the exact sciences at any rate—has not been the deletion and replacement of religious ideas, but rather the assimilation and reinterpretation of religious ideas, as constitutive elements in a world view founded on secular premises. Much of what distinguishes writers I call "Romantic" derives from the fact that they undertook, whatever their religious creed or lack of creed, to save traditional concepts, schemes and values which had been based on the relation of the Creator to his creature and creation, but to reformulate them within the prevailing two-term system of subject and object, ego and non-ego, the human mind or consciousness and its transactions with nature. (13)

Abrams intends, of course, to discredit the idea that Romantic writers simply jettisoned tradition and turned directly to nature and immediate personal experience as their source of imaginative strength. But the force of his own position goes beyond the claim that there is a wide-ranging network of correspondences linking Romantic thought to "the centuries old Judeo-Christian culture" out of which it emerged. More emphatically, the thrust of Abrams's account is to portray Romanticism as in its very essence an interpretation or reading of that tradition. The interpretive engagement of Romantic writers with biblical texts and inherited modes of religious thought is, he implies, not simply the means by which they arrived at a more or less autonomous system of thought; rather, that engagement is the condition of their activity as writers and thinkers.

Given this premise, let us examine more closely how Abrams distinguishes the Romantic interpretation of biblical tradition from earlier interpretations. His argument, in outline, is that Romanticism is an *internalization* of biblically sanctioned modes of thought and, more specifically, of the historical scheme of creation, fall, and millennial redemption that Abrams presents as definitive of Judeo-Christian thought: in Romanticism, the "design of biblical history" (12) becomes reinterpreted as a drama of consciousness, with the human imagination replacing supernatural intervention as the agency of redemption. Since Abrams is well aware that the history of biblical exegesis offers many instances of comparable interpretative tendencies, he further specifies that the events of the French Revolution and its aftermath, in their awakening and betrayal of millennial hopes, played a crucial mediating role in the development of Romantic thought. "Romantic literature," Abrams writes, "differs from [its] theological precedents in that its recourse is from one secular means of renovating the world to another. To put the matter with the sharpness of drastic simplification: faith in an apocalypse by revelation is replaced by faith in apocalypse by revolution, and this now gave way to faith in an apocalypse by imagination and cognition" (334).

As Abrams acknowledges, the clarity of this account may be gained at the cost of oversimplification. Is millennial thinking as distinctive of Judeo-Christian tradition as Abrams claims? Is that tradition as internally homogeneous as he intimates? To raise only the most obvious question, are Jewish and Christian concepts of biblical history fundamentally equivalent, as Abrams implies in speaking globally of the "biblical design of history"? Is it clear that Romanticism is a response to the French Revolution rather than the other way around? What of Rousseau, for example, arguably the key figure of European Romanticism, who died in 1778, some eleven years before the outbreak of the Revolution, and whom Abrams, limiting himself to cultural developments in England and Germany, largely neglects? Has Abrams, in fact, sufficiently distinguished Romanticism as an internalization of the scheme of biblical history from its theological precedents? Insofar as *Natural Supernaturalism* avoids squarely confronting these issues, the strength of the book lies in the wealth of historical material it assembles and collocates rather than in the schematic framework it uses to organize that material.

At the same time, it must be emphasized that the schema of cultural history employed in *Natural Supernaturalism* is by no means peculiar to

Abrams. On the contrary, his recourse to the dialectics of internalization as a principle of historical articulation reflects a treatment of Romanticism that is both time honored and widely accepted. In Hegel's historical aesthetic system, for example, which conceptualizes a development from symbolic through classical to romantic art, romantic art is said to resemble symbolic art (which includes, for Hegel, representations of God in the Hebrew Bible) in that for both—in contrast to classical art—the Idea has no adequate material expression. They differ, however, in that for symbolic art the Idea transcends human consciousness and is therefore abstract and "defective," whereas for romantic art the idea is immanent in human consciousness itself. Thus Hegel writes in the introduction to the *Aesthetics:* "In the sphere of the Romantic, the Idea, whose defectiveness in the case of the symbol produced the defect of external shape, has to reveal itself in the medium of spirit and feelings as perfected in itself. And it is because of this higher perfection that it withdraws itself from any adequate union with the external element" (117). The affinities with Abrams's account are limited by the fact, among others, that for Hegel romantic art comes into being with the advent of Christianity, but this divergence in views is, as will emerge, less decisive than it may seem.

On the assumption that any attitude held in common by Abrams and Derrida is, a fortiori, widely shared, I would also cite in this connection the description in *De la grammatologie* of Rousseau's treatment of the relation between writing and presence as a "modification tout intérieure du schéma platonicien" [wholly interior modification of the Platonic schema] (30).[2] Rousseau plays an exemplary role in Derrida's historical account precisely because he "repeats the Platonic gesture" of subjugating writing to the manifestation of presence in the logos, "while referring to another model of presence, self-presence through feeling, through the palpable cogito that simultaneously carries within itself the inscription of the divine law" (30). Again the parallel with Abrams is not exact, since the schema Rousseau's work internalizes is Platonic rather than biblical. But Derrida himself blurs this distinction when he goes on to cite in support of his claims the following passage from Rousseau: "La Bible est le plus sublime de tous les livres . . . mais enfin c'est un livre . . . ce n'est point sur quelque feuilles éparses qu'il faut aller chercher la loi de Dieu, mais dans le coeur de l'homme où sa main daigna l'écrire" [The Bible is the most sublime of books . . . but in the end it is a book . . . it is not on some scattered leaves that one should seek God's law, but in the heart of man where his hand deigned to write it] ("Lettre à Vernes," cited in *De la grammatologie* 29).

These accounts differ as to when Romanticism assumes its cultural hegemony and as to what tradition or traditions of thought it assimilates, but they concur in treating Romanticism both as a historical development and as a particular mode of rhetorical transformation—what I have been calling "internalization." It is this articulation of history and rhetoric that I now want to examine more closely.

APART from its associations with a particular historical moment, the schema of internalization, as it is applied by the writers I have referred to, presupposes a certain temporalizing of spatial oppositions. In the case of Abrams, for whom internalization is basically a mode of analogical construction, this is not immediately obvious. Since Abrams is primarily interested in exhibiting correspondences and continuities, he tends to alternate between a diachronic account and a synchronic perspective that examines the structural correspondences between the moments of the historical sequence, while abstracting from the temporal aspect of their relationship. (Thus, for example, the relation between "secular" and "sacred" in *Natural Supernaturalism* is sometimes a matter of historical derivation, sometimes a matter of structural opposition.) Yet the narrative form of his argument dictates that the relation between theocentric and psychological interpretative orientations be understood as successive and not simply complementary. The internalized analogical derivative of biblical history is presented not simply as supplementing the account it derives from, but as taking its place, assuming its authority as a totalizing representation.

The implications of thus temporalizing the relation between outer and inner may be clarified by an example borrowed from Dante's exposition of the fourfold scheme of biblical exegesis in his letter to Can Grande della Scala. Taking as his text the opening verses of Psalm 114 ("When Israel went out of Egypt, the house of Jacob from a people of strange language; Judah was his sanctuary, and Israel his dominion"), Dante distinguishes between the "historical or literal" sense, which he defines as "the departure of the children of Israel from Egypt in the time of Moses," and the "moral" sense, which is "the conversion of the soul from the grief and misery of sin to the state of grace." The relation between these two readings seems analogical: Egypt is to the land of Israel as the state of sin is to the state of grace. There seems to be no intrinsic need to choose between them or to order them hierarchically. The situation is complicated, however, by the inclusion within Dante's interpretative system of an "allegorical" reading (we would speak of a typological reading)[3] that expounds the sense of the passage as "our redemption wrought by Christ." Since Christ's advent marks, among other things and perhaps primarily, the deliverance of the word from its bondage to the historical understanding, this interpretation effectively transforms the text into an allegory prescriptive of its own reading. The relation of this allegorical reading to the literal meaning of the text can no longer be construed as analogical. (Since within the Christian fourfold scheme the moral sense is founded on the allegorical or typological sense, the analogical reading is based on the allegorical reading and not the other way around, although I have presented them in the reverse order for purposes of exposition.)

The same pattern of complication may be illustrated less anachronistically by reference to Keats's "The Fall of Hyperion," a dream poem that has usually been read as an allegory of Keats's poetic development.[4] The narrative opens with a description of Keats standing in a bower amid the opulent "refuse of a meal / By angel tasted, or our Mother Eve." Apart from this implicit reference to the garden of Eden, the passage is strongly marked by allusions to *Paradise Lost,* though interestingly, as the lines cited indicate, Keats conflates references to Eve's partaking of the forbidden fruit with references to the meal she serves to Raphael.[5]

The most striking aspect of Keats's reworking of his sources, however, is the introduction of the poet himself as a figure within the Edenic enclosure.[6] Keats is not in a garden that is "like" the garden of Eden but is in the very place itself, almost as though he had wandered onto a set after the scene had been shot but before the props had been cleared away. The bold movement by which Keats imaginatively projects himself into the vacated space of the precursor text is, at the same time, an *internalization* of his Miltonic and biblical sources in that he subsumes their epic or mythic scenes within an autobiographical dream narrative of a dream. The point I want to emphasize, however, is that the poem not only enacts this subsumption but allegorically narrates that enactment: no sooner does the poet project himself into this slightly used but in good condition paradise than he repeats Eve's fatal error—Keats eats.

> And appetite
> More yearning than on earth I ever felt
> Growing within, I ate deliciously;
> And, after not long, thirsted, for thereby
> Stood a cool vessel of transparent juice,
> Sipp'd by the wander'd bee, *the which I took,*
> *And pledging all the mortals of the world,*

And all the dead whose names are in our lips,
Drank. That full draught is parent of my theme.
No Asian poppy, nor elixir fine
Of the soon fading jealous Caliphat;
No poison gender'd in close monkish cell
To thin the scarlet conclave of old men
Could so have rapt unwilling life away.
Among the fragrant husks and berries crush'd,
Upon the grass I struggled hard against
The domineering potion; but in vain—
The cloudy swoon came on, and down I sunk
Like a Silenus on an antique vase.   (1.38–56; emphasis added)

The peculiar density of these lines can best be appreciated if we compare them with a closely related passage that occurs just before the sudden breaking off of Keats's first "Hyperion." In this passage the young Apollo—clearly the poet's surrogate in Keats's ambition to inherit Milton's "epic grandeur"—addresses the goddess Mnemosyne, who has come to summon him to his new station as Hyperion's successor:

Mute thou remainest—mute! yet I can read
A wondrous lesson in thy silent face:
Knowledge enormous makes a God of me.
Names, deeds, gray legends, dire events, rebellions,
Majesties, sovran voices, agonies,
Creations and destroyings, all at once
Pour into the wide hollows of my brain,
And deify me, as if some blithe wine
Or bright elixir peerless I had drunk
And so become immortal.   (3.111–20)

Both passages dramatize a fateful initiation (cf. "That full draught is parent of my theme"). But in the passage from the earlier poem this process is imagined primarily as one of mental internalization ("Names, deeds . . . Pour into . . . my brain") and is only metaphorically likened to a material process of ingestion ("as if some . . . bright elixir . . . I had drunk"). Concomitantly, this process expands consciousness ("Knowledge enormous makes a God of me") as the "wide hollows" of Apollo's brain become the repository of all history and tradition. As in Abrams's model of Romantic internalization, the dominant pattern here is one of transposition: very roughly, Hyperion is to

Apollo as Milton is to Keats. The passage from "The Fall of Hyperion," by contrast, is much more focused on the hermetic, allegorical elaboration of the material figure of ingestion and culminates not in the expansion of consciousness but in its loss: "The cloudy swoon came on, and down I sunk." As in the example from Dante, the precursor text—here the story of the fall—functions specifically as an allegory prescriptive of its own reading, and as such it figures as an element within the narrative it prescribes: the internalized narrative is thus itself a narrative of internalization. The dense proliferation within this passage of objects and acts of ingestion points up their overdetermined status. On the one hand, they function as figures for the process of internalizing citation; on the other hand, they reflect the unassimilated persistence of the figure thus cited. Like the concept of internalization as analyzed in chapter 1, they thus mark a contingent but ineluctable point of contact between a movement of self-reflection and the material in which it is absorbed.

I have sought by these examples to illustrate the involuted nature of the relation between rhetorical patterns of internalization and the critical discourse about these patterns, contrasting this complexity with the seeming clarity of Abrams's historical account, itself a function of his reliance on analogical models. Let me now attempt a more general description. The peculiar complexity and power of internalizing allegorical readings derives from their functioning both as interpretations of a text and as metacritical statements regulating the text's interpretation. Such a reading thus effectively confounds the question of its own interpretative validity (its truth as a representation of the meaning of the text) with the question of the text's referential authority (its truth as a representation of the world). It is as though the authority of the text was such that the rules governing its reading had themselves to be derived from a reading of the text, a reading that would be possible only insofar as it was already guided by the rules it was seeking to enunciate.

The element of circularity or discontinuity implied by this situation is indeed to some extent implicit in all interpretation, since statements about what a text means always interact with claims concerning its referential orientation and degree of internal coherence. What distinguishes self-reflexive, internalizing readings is the way they systematically condense a pervasive hermeneutic condition in a single moment of interpretative crisis.[7] Forcing this moment of crisis does not resolve the interpretative difficulties, which are insuperable, but it does render them, like Kafka's leopards in the temple, calculable in advance.[8] The interference of functions that blocks access to the meaning of the text thus becomes contained within a narrative that moves from an "understanding" of the text—which is in fact a misunderstanding—via a pivotal moment of inscrutability to its own negative understanding of that inscrutability.

Since the internalizing reading of the text as the narrative of a process of self-understanding is in essence metacritical, it follows that any critical discourse about patterns of internalization will inevitably be implicated, more or less coherently, in the rhetorical transformations it describes. Thus, for example, in Abrams's account of the historical process by which the biblical story of the fall cedes its place to an internalized, secularized version of that story, one may trace in outline precisely such a secularized version of the fall. And this means that not only the narrative pattern of *Natural Supernaturalism* but its very historical character is determined rhetorically (as the transformation of another symbolic structure) before it is determined referentially. More specifically, by portraying the internalization of scriptural authority as an event belonging to a more or less definite historical period, Abrams underscores the contrast on which his account of tradition depends: between a transhistorical core of Scripture and the shifting interpretations of that core. Yet at the same time the story he tells is the story of the undoing of that opposition. The historiography of Romanticism thus both registers the paradoxes of textual authority and contains them by narrativizing and historicizing them. It enacts a supplementary repression of residual problems in the attempt to distinguish sharply between scriptural and literary authority, an attempt that is itself undertaken as a means of adjusting tensions within the more general concept of textual authority.

Up to this point I have primarily been analyzing a certain critical-historical account of Romanticism, stressing the paradoxes and involutions that account entails. It remains to be asked, however, whether Romanticism's implicit understanding of itself and of its relation to "Scripture" poses the same problems. Our brief consideration of a passage from "The Fall of Hyperion" suggested that within limits this may be so, but to pursue the question further we must undertake a more detailed reading of a Romantic text.

THE POEM I have chosen to discuss, Wordsworth's "My Heart Leaps Up," offers the advantage of occupying both a central position in the canon and a marginal position in Wordsworthian criticism. Its centrality is attested to by the fact, noted by Frances Ferguson (*Wordsworth,* 40) and by F. W. Bateson (*Wordsworth,* 40), that in all the editions of Wordsworth's collected poems that he himself supervised it is the opening poem and also by its hold on the public memory. Its marginality can be confirmed by a survey of the critical literature: it is occasionally referred to in passing, but except for the concluding three lines, which Wordsworth was to incorporate as the epigraph to the "Immortality Ode," it is virtually never read.[9] One need not, I believe, look far for the reasons behind this critical neglect. The extreme simplicity, even by Wordsworth's standards, of the diction and statement of much of the poem do not invite—some would say merit—further comment. Bateson speaks of "those now almost all too familiar lines" (*Wordsworth,* 41), but one suspects they may have always seemed so. Yet the very discrepancy between the poem's critical and canonical standings is itself of interest in that it may reflect a power of utterance in Romantic writing that the dominant critical understanding has difficulty engaging. Here is the text:

> My heart leaps up when I behold
> A rainbow in the sky:
> So was it when my life began;
> So is it now I am a man;
> So be it when I shall grow old,
> Or let me die!
> The Child is father of the Man;
> And I could wish my days to be
> Bound each to each by natural piety.

Let me first emphasize the sacramental aspects of the poem. Its generic mode, insofar as it can be precisely characterized, seems to be that of a creed, that is to say, an iterable (and easily memorized) testimony of faith. (Here again its place in the collected poems is relevant.) More obviously, its explicit theme is "natural piety," a locution that invites comparison with "natural supernaturalism," the phrase Abrams borrowed from Carlyle for the title of his book. At the same time, as the poem's final words remind us, Wordsworth's frame of reference is resolutely natural and subjective. If there is a power that binds together first and last things, it is a power in nature and in human feeling, and the first and last things are preeminently those of one person's life. The poem thus indeed seems to naturalize the supernatural and to internalize the transcendent, subsuming inherited religious ideas and patterns within a secular outlook.

This perspective also provides a rationale for the Wordsworthian "naturalizing" of poetic language of which "My Heart Leaps Up" is a prime specimen. The tendency to avoid salient figuration and, more specifically, allegorical diction (in the Coleridgean sense of allegory in its opposition to symbol) would express the poet's rejection of a prior textual authority interposed between himself and nature or himself and the reader, while the implicit belief in the naturalness and universality of Wordsworth's subjective responses would compensate poetically for the relinquished appeal to scriptural authority. The significance of the poem and the aura of its language would derive not simply from its literal statement, but from the seamless integration of that statement with the expression of a subjective, universal truth.[10]

A reading of the poem along these lines could be pursued in greater detail and could be reinforced by reference to a great many other Romantic texts. Nonetheless, the apparent transparency and availability of the poem's language is riddled with complexities that are not easily resolved within the framework of a reading like the one as I have so far presented. Most obviously, the famous aphorism of line 7, "The Child is father of the Man," which the poem dramatically foregrounds, has an enigmatic, almost oracular force, which persists whatever we may finally decide the line means, and which is directly related to the line's chiasmic scrambling of that normative sequence par excellence: man/subject fathers/verb child/object. Similarly, if less conspicuously, the qualifying force of "I could wish my days to be . . ." is puzzling in a way that borders on agrammaticality. Again, the grammatical and rhythmic parallelism of lines 3–5 ("So was it . . . So is it . . . So be it . . .") articulating the continuity of past, present, and future, while in itself quite natural and simple, is also oddly arch and artful if we consider that it is intended as a syntactic equivalent for the opening image of the rainbow, a connection reinforced by the latent pun by which the rainbow is made to bind together the poet's days. On a more general level, the rhythm of the poem is highly irregular (consider, for example, the rhythmic condensation of line 6, "Or let me die!" or the broken-backed pentameter of the final line), and its discursive movement is disjointed. (What, for instance, is the logical force of the "And" connecting lines 8 and 9 to line 7?)

But from our perspective the most significant of the factors complicating the texture of "My Heart Leaps Up" is the latent allusion to Genesis 9 that may be said to underlie the entire poem: "I do set my bow in the cloud, and it shall be for a token of a covenant between me and the earth." Indeed, our entire reading of the poem and, more broadly, the theoretical and historical debate we are involved in may be organized around the assessment of this allusion. There is little need to argue about whether the allusion is intended. Given such a blanket acknowledgment of indebtedness as Wordsworth's statement in the 1815 Preface to his *Collected Poems*, "The grand store-houses of enthusiastic and meditative imagination . . . in these unfavorable times are the prophetic and lyrical parts of the Holy Scriptures, and the works of Milton" (*Selected Poems and Prefaces*, 486), the burden of proof rests with the critic who wishes to deny the relevance of the allusion. What should concern us here is the nature of that relevance.

Although this specific question has until recently been largely neglected by the critical tradition, Abrams himself has commented briefly on the allusion, not in *Natural Supernaturalism* but in the *Norton Anthology of Literature*, where he glosses "natural piety" as follows: "As distinguished from piety based on the Scriptures, in which God makes the rainbow the token of his covenant with Noah and all his descendants. The religious sentiment that binds Wordsworth's mature self to that of his childhood is a continuing responsiveness to the miracle of ordinary things" (2:212).[11] In this view, the function of the allusion is contradistinguishing: the specific meaning of "natural piety" is clarified by the play of analogy and difference operating between the biblical text and the poem, a reading that is obviously congruent with the central theses of *Natural Supernaturalism*. But if this is true, that Wordsworth articulates a creed of natural piety by way of a scriptural allusion becomes highly problematic, since the claim to immediacy of experience and to a power of poetic utterance inspired by that immediacy, rather than by the transmitted authority of a tradition, is itself mediated by a reference to that tradition.

Abrams's reading here again points to complications and ambivalences it does not confront. Let me sharpen the issue by falling back, at first, on a familiar vocabulary of linguistic analysis. We say that the word "rainbow" has, to begin with, a certain denotative value, referring to a certain natural object/event/illusion that appears under certain conditions, is many colored, is shaped like a broken or unbroken arc, and so on. Furthermore, the word has a range of connotative values based on the experiences we associate with seeing a rainbow. Although these connotations are subjective—we can imagine, as Wordsworth does, seeing a rainbow and not having these feelings—they may nonetheless be universal, in keeping with Kant's conception of aesthetic judgment as involving a claim to subjective universality.[12] On the other hand, the word has connotations that derive from its inscription within the biblical narrative of the flood; these connotations are based not on the direct experience of a natural phenomenon, but rather on the transmission of a very specific scriptural legacy. From this point of view, the problem of understanding the allusion to Genesis in "My Heart Leaps Up" would be that of understanding the relation between these two potentially conflicting orders of connotation.

We may receive guidance in navigating this problem from Geoffrey Hartman's observation that the untimeliness or excessive force of line 6, which formalizes and dramatizes the poem's status as an oath (and which may be read, I propose, as a transformation of the common law formula, "So help me God"), "becomes timely again when we recall [the] utterance . . . of the creator when he makes the rainbow a sign of His bond" (*Unremarkable Wordsworth*, 157).[13] As I have noted, there is indeed something slightly "off" about the whole poem, and from this point of view the scriptural recollection is untimely insofar as it interposes itself between the poet and the appeal to a spontaneous movement of early response unmediated by scriptural associations. Yet poem and proof text never set themselves in opposition: we cannot say that the recollection of the biblical text disturbs the synchronization of the poem's moment of utterance with the impulse it recalls, because this relationship is already disturbed. Rather, the recollection accommodates the agitations of Wordsworth's language not by countering them with a more stable and authoritative power of utterance, but by giving them scope and in particular by relieving the pressure to collapse language and experience into a single authoritative moment.

Seen in this way, it becomes clearer that both texts—Genesis and "My Heart Leaps Up"—challenge the adequacy of the linguistic and cognitive distinctions we have thus far relied on in seeking to understand their relation and that consequently everything depends here on the nuances of reading as they resist the mastery of this conceptual framework. Consider the biblical text. God's covenant with the earth is in fact expressed in two forms: first it is uttered ("And I, behold, I establish my covenant with you, and with your seed after you"), and then God decrees that the rainbow will be the sign of this promise. In other words, first there is an oral promise and then God, as it were, puts it in writing—a kind of magic writing, as ephemeral as the spoken word yet more persistent, in the unpredictability of its recurrence, than an inscription. Thus the institution of the rainbow as the sign of the covenant is not the institution of an arbitrary mark or sign, whose meaning is codified by a divine decree preserved in the Bible; rather the institution of meaning is limited or conditioned in a certain way by the physical properties of the sign. This sense of limitation is further underlined in that the rainbow not only will remind man of God's promise, but will remind God himself: "And the bow shall be in the cloud; and I will look upon it, that I may remember the everlasting covenant between God and every living creature of all flesh that is upon the earth."

The implication that God could forget his promise is hardly reassuring, but it is also in keeping with the fragility and intermittence of the rainbow sign. What our recollection of Scripture brings to the reading of "My Heart Leaps Up" is the sense that the speaker is responding to a kind of promise and also to a tacit awareness of the fragility of both promise and response. The precise origin and meaning of the promise remain unspecified: the speaker's movement of response is as much a sign as the rainbow itself, and the promise he responds to is simply that in the future he will be able to respond to that promise. It has no fulfillment other than in its repetition.[14] The experience "My Heart Leaps Up" is concerned with, then, is not a moment of unmediated perceptual intensity, but an experience of time as pure repetition in which it is impossible to distinguish sensation, memory, and anticipation from one other.

Wordsworth's poem both does and does not offer itself as a repetition of the scriptural promise it recalls. Formally, the poem is a promise or vow ("So be it when I shall grow old, / Or let me die!"). But it is unclear to whom this promise is addressed, and the very need to promise introduces an element of doubt and anxiety that is allowed further expression in the restrained wish and uncertain meter of the closing lines. Shall we say that it is these hesitations that distinguish Wordsworth's poetic affirmations from the authority claimed by Scripture? It is to precisely this question that the poem offers its quickening, yet hesitant, response.

CHAPTER
'Three

Monster Feedback

Retrospection, Traumatic Internalization,
and Perceptual Aberration in *Prelude* 1

C hapter 2 was concerned primarily with internalization as a recurrent figure in literary histories of European Romanticism,
beginning with the histories Romanticism offers of itself. This chapter carries that discussion onto a more psychoanalytic terrain, where internalization figures in the psychic history of the individual, most characteristically
with regard to the development of the conscience. This shift of focus is not
secured by any clear-cut analogical relation between the two dimensions of
concern, "ontogeny recapitulating phylogeny." But neither is it wholly discontinuous, if only because the psychic history our discussion will revolve
around is that of a Romantic writer fully sensible to the interpenetration of
his own history and that of his age.

Accordingly the first part of this chapter, though taking Wordsworth as
its point of departure, is devoted primarily to the strategic assembly of citations from three related and highly influential modern accounts of the role
internalization plays in developing the sense of guilt: those of Nietzsche,
Freud, and Melanie Klein. I aim to retrace the basic lineaments of these accounts and show their affinity with Wordsworth's recounting of "the growth
of the poet's mind." But in doing so, I also emphasize an aspect of structural
complexity or contingency in the psychoanalytic accounts that I referred in
the introduction to this collection and that is, in my view, too often missing
from current debates about the social construction of the subject.

The second section returns to Wordsworth, though not yet to an actual
reading, to suggest how the psychoanalytic meditation on internalization
and guilt may be connected to a problem more specific to the rhetoric and

epistemology of autobiographical narrative, that of "projecting backward" as it relates to the question of the text's referentiality, its anchorage in a pre-existing state of affairs.[1] Finally, I turn to a reading of what is commonly referred to as the boat-stealing episode in book 1 of *The Prelude* (see appendix C), a poetic narrative in which guilt, projecting backward, and traumatic internalization are all prominently thematized, with a brief detour through another story from *Prelude* 1 about theft, guilt, projection, and internalization. Not for nothing has Alan Liu pointed specifically to these episodes to substantiate his suggestively ambiguous claim that "poetic criminality was in excess of criminal history" (*Wordsworth and the Sense of History*, 226), an observation that warrants comparison with Freud's repeated assertion that the superego's "excessive severity does not follow a real model" (*Standard Edition*, 23:206).

THAT WORDSWORTH himself viewed the boat-stealing episode as emblematic of the process that shaped his "poetic conscience" is clear from the rapturous apostrophe that follows the narrative:

> Wisdom and spirit of the universe,
> Thou soul that art the eternity of thought,
> That giv'st to forms and images a breath
> And everlasting motion—not in vain,
> By day or star-light thus from my first dawn
> Of childhood didst thou intertwine for me
> The passions that build up our human soul,
> Not with the mean and vulgar works of man,
> But with high objects, with enduring things,
> With life and Nature, purifying thus
> The elements of feeling and of thought,
> And sanctifying by such discipline
> Both pain and fear, until we recognise
> A grandeur in the beatings of the heart.   (427–41)

Although the "thus" of line 431 encompasses in its reach all the childhood experiences Wordsworth has recounted up to this point, and though in its earliest versions this passage did not directly follow the boat-stealing episode, its generalizing diction maps onto the details of that episode in suggestively literal ways. Specifically, the "mean and vulgar works of man" correlate with the shepherd's skiff that lures the boy into the scene, while the "high objects

... enduring things ... life ... and nature" that enlarge and elevate his passions recall the towering and quasi-hallucinatory "grim shape" that looms up out of the landscape and continues to haunt Wordsworth's thoughts and dreams long after he has left the scene—even to the time of the lines' writing. More obliquely but not less crucially, the "grandeur in the beatings of the heart" that we are to recognize recalls in sublimated fashion the pounding terror whose pulsations drive the child's efforts at flight at the same time that they flood and animate the phantasmagoric encounter:

> ... I struck and struck again,
> And growing still in stature, the huge cliff
> Rose up between me and the stars, and still,
> With measured motion, like a living thing,
> Strode after me.   (408–11)

Bearing these points of attachment in mind, and pausing only to note the rhetorical and grammatical modulation of the passage from a strongly hieratic "I-thou" axis of address to an encompassing "we,"[2] we may observe that the transfer and transformation Wordsworth recounts involves not only a movement from low to high but also, in a shift that is more difficult to picture and that depends both on the mediation of pain and fear and on the ambiguities of the word "grandeur," from "high objects" to "the beatings of the heart"—that is, from outer to inner. Some time ago, Colin Clarke characterized this passage as "ingenious double-talk," and the way "grandeur" functions here as a switch word between the lofty in its opposition to the low and the expanded in its opposition to the contracted seems to instance his point. The question remains, however, whether something like that verbal relay is not itself a constitutive element in the formative process for which Wordsworth's language seeks to secure recognition.

Let us now relate the moral and aesthetic psychology of these lines, as they engage with the experience whose narration they follow, to the accounts alluded to earlier concerning the origins of the sense of guilt. Since the nature of these accounts could in each case furnish the occasion for extended discussion, I will limit myself to citing a few touchstone passages in which each writer offers a lapidary statement of his or her argument.

From Nietzsche we may consider the following summary comment from *Ecce Homo* on the second essay of *Zur Genealogie der Moral* ("'Schuld,' 'Schlectes Gewissen' und Verwandtes" ["'Guilt,' 'bad conscience,' and the like"]):

Die *zweite* Abhandlung gibt die Psychologie des *Gewissens:* dasselbe ist *nicht,* wie wohl geglaubt wird, "die Stimme Gottes im Menschen"—es ist der Instinkt der Grausamkeit, der sich zückwärts wendet, nachdem er nicht mehr nach aussen hin sich entladen kann.

[The *second* inquiry offers the psychology of the *conscience*—which is not, as people may believe, "the voice of God in man": it is the instinct of cruelty that turns back after it can no longer discharge itself externally.] (*Werke,* 2:1143; Kaufmann translation, 312)

The language of this passage harks back most directly to a particular paragraph in the second essay, whose first and last sentences read as follows:

Alle Instinkte, welche sich nicht nach aussen entladen, *wenden sich nach innen*—dies ist das, was ich die *Verinnerlichung* des Menschen nenne: damit wächst erst das an den Menschen heran, was man später seine "Seele" nennt. . . . Die Feindschaft, die Grausamkeit, die Lust an der Verflügung, am Überfall, am Wechsel, an der Zerstörung—alles das gegen die Inhaber solcher Instinkte sich wendend: *das* ist der Ursprung des "schlecten Gewissens."

[All instincts that do not discharge themselves outwardly *turn inward*—this is what I call the *internalization* of man: thus it was that man first developed what was later called his "soul." . . . Hostility, cruelty, joy in persecuting, in attacking, in change, in destruction—all this turned against the possessors of such instincts: *that* is the origin of the "bad conscience."] (*Werke,* 2:825; Kaufmann translation, 84–85)

Nietzsche's thesis is an important precursor, and no doubt at least in part a source, of Freud's evolving account of the origins of the superego.[3] Consider this passage from Freud's last major writing, *An Outline of Psychoanalysis:*

A portion of the external world has, at least partially, been abandoned as an object and has instead, by identification, been taken into the ego and thus become an integral part of the internal world. . . .We call this agency the super-ego and are aware of it in its judicial functions as our conscience. It is a remarkable thing that the super-ego often displays a severity for which no model has been provided by the real parent. . . . The super-ego is in fact the heir to the Oedipus complex and is only established after that complex has been disposed of. For that reason its excessive severity does not follow a real model but corresponds to the strength of the defense used against the temptation of the Oedipus complex. Some suspicion of this state of things lies, no doubt, at the bottom of the assertion made by philosophers and believers that the moral sense is not instilled in men by education or acquired by them in their social life but is implanted in them from a higher source. (*Standard Edition*, 23:205–6)

The quasi-technical reference in this passage to "the strength of the defense used against the temptation of the Oedipus complex" may be elucidated by the following passage from *Civilization and Its Discontents*, which also reinforces the connections with Nietzsche:

What happens in the history of the development of the individual to render his desire for aggression innocuous? Something very remarkable, which we should never have guessed and which is nevertheless quite obvious. His aggression is introjected, internalized; it is, in point of fact, sent back to where it came from—that is, it is directed towards his own ego. There it is taken over by a portion of the ego, which sets itself over against the rest of the ego as super-ego, and which now, in the form of "conscience," is ready to put into action against the ego the same harsh aggressiveness that the ego would have liked to satisfy upon other, extraneous individuals. (23:123)

Oedipal interpretations of the boat-stealing episode are by now common fare;[4] nor would anyone seeking to debunk the importance Freud accords to castration anxiety within the playing out of the Oedipal scenario be well advised to make Wordsworth's story about his "elfin pinnace" (as he calls the boat) the proving ground for a counterargument. But my initial purpose in citing these passages from Freud and juxtaposing them with those from Nietzsche is not to prepare yet another rehearsal of that reading (though I will of necessity be referring to it when I address Wordsworth's narrative more directly), or to draw without reservation on their notions of primal aggressivity (insofar as these are used to subordinate a multiplicity of conditioning factors to a single formative confrontation between nature and culture or desire and the law). It is rather to highlight something about the psychoanalytic concept of internalization that emerges with particular clarity from the juxtaposition. For in these passages the process of internalization exhibits two aspects. On the one hand, it involves the picture of the transfer of a powerful object—in Freud's account, the father as prohibitive authority—from an outer to an inner sphere. (And "outer" and "inner" here mean exactly that; they are not metaphors—for example, for "public" and "private"—but rudimentary ways of mapping difference and change that cover, and cover over, a wide range of relationships.) On the other hand, "internalization" calls up the picture of a force arising from within and seeking to discharge itself externally—whether in speech or in deed—but thwarted in its initial thrust and directed back toward its source. This dimension of meaning is stressed in Nietzsche's account, but it is clearly important in Freud's as well, and one cannot begin to do justice to Freud's meditations on superego formation if one does not bear in mind that it involves a moment of contingent articulation between these two shaping factors.

We find a similar articulation—not surprisingly, since Freud cites her work in expounding his own theory—in the following bravura formulation from Melanie Klein's "Contribution to the Psychogenesis of Manic-Depressive States":

> The development of the infant is governed by the mechanisms of introjection and projection. From the beginning the ego introjects objects "good" and "bad," for both of which its mother's breast is the prototype—for good objects when the child obtains it and for bad when it fails him. But it is because the baby projects its own aggression on to these objects that it feels them to be "bad" and not only in that they frustrate its desires: the child conceives of them as actually dangerous—persecutors who it fears will devour it, scoop out the inside of its body, cut it to pieces, poison it—in short, compassing its destruction by all the means which sadism can devise. (282)

Although Klein is offering here her account of normal infantile paranoia, it is the realization in fantasy of the infant's oral sadistic impulses toward the object that precipitates feelings of guilt (following on the realization that the object of love and the object of hate are one) and the subsequent work of reparation.[5] As in Freud's account, the parent is both actually frustrating and a mirror of the child's malignant fury, but this time the story is focused not on the father as embodiment of social authority and target of aggression but rather on the mother, and more specifically the maternal breast. Correlatively, Klein seeks to reimagine those processes of "primary" internalization and externalization by which boundaries between inner and outer, self and other, coalesce in the first place. The relation between these Oedipal and pre-Oedipal scenarios will concern us later. For the moment I want only to emphasize yet again the compounded nature of the process Klein describes and the variability of the relation between passion and object that emerges from a comparison of these two founding psychoanalytic accounts.

THE PERTINENCE of these very general considerations to a reading of the boat-stealing incident remains to be explored. By way of transition, let us now shift our focus from these modern rewritings of the mythological origins of guilt (in the Bible too, of course, a story about an "internalization") to a more manifestly literary problem. There is ample evidence, ranging from early manuscript material (the earliest versions of the boat-stealing episode predate the emergence of *The Prelude* as a conscious project) to the eventual positioning of the episode within the unfolding structure of *Prelude* 1, that in drafting these lines Wordsworth was testing the reach of his power as a writer. For at roughly the same time, and with Coleridge urging him along, he is vaunting his ambition to write a vast philosophical poem "On Man, on Nature, and on Human Life" that will pass "Jehovah" (read Milton), "with his thunder, and the quire of shouting angels . . . unalarmed" ("Prospectus to *The Recluse*"), an ambition whose thwarting precipitates self-doubts:

> Was it for this
> That one, the fairest of all rivers, loved
> To blend his murmurs with my nurse's song . . .   (271–73)[6]

Both ambition and anxiety are projected backward then onto this recollection of a boyhood appropriation of a vehicle that turns into a trial of powers ("And now, as suited one who proudly rowed with his best skill"). Apart from the near homonymy of "boat" and "poet," one encounters, particularly in the open lines of the episode, a fairly dense trail of allusion, first to Milton and then to Coleridge. Thus "Even like a man who walks with stately step / Though bent on speed" repeats almost verbatim a line and a half from the beginning of book 12 of *Paradise Lost*, "as one who in his journey bates at noon, though bent on speed" (Norton edition, 48n).[7] while the "tracks of shining white" left by the water snakes in "The Rime of the Ancient Mariner" (274) resurface in the "track of sparkling light" (366–67) the child leaves in his wake (Maxwell edition, 541n) and the Mariner's spellbinding "glittering eye" turns up immediately before in the phrase "small circles glittering idly in the moon."

At a more generic level, the passage engages "Lycidas" and the conventions of pastoral elegy in a particularly fraught way. In "Wordsworth's Whelming Tide: Coleridge and the Art of Analogy," Reeve Parker has discussed the significant role "Lycidas" played in the dynamics of Wordsworth's and Coleridge's interaction at this time (*Coleridge's Meditative Art,* 221–39)—readers may infer who drowns—and here I propose a related tack. Within the Virgilian tradition that Milton was drawing on, the pastoral elegy was itself a form in which the aspiring poet prepared himself for work of epic scope, so that the boat-stealing episode may be seen as both invoking and transforming this program of poetic initiation. The most obvious transformation would be that Wordsworth puts himself in the boat, thus making pastoral elegy into a frankly autobiographical narrative, or in the idiom of this book, internalizing its terms. Within this allegory of literary history, the shepherd's skiff figures as the synecdoche of "Lycidas," and Wordsworth's "act of stealth" corresponds to the appropriation of pastoral convention under the guise of autobiographical recollection. Consider, for example, how the following central moment in "Lycidas," a moment that deals explicitly with questions of poetic ambition and recognition, reverberates at a comparably pivotal moment in Wordsworth's text:

> Fame is the spur that the clear spirit doth raise
> (That last infirmity of Noble mind)
> To scorn delights, and live laborious days;
> But the fair Guerdon when we hope to find,
> And think to burst out into sudden blaze,
> Comes the blind Fury with th' abhorred shears,
> And slits the thin-spun life. "But not the praise,"
> Phoebus repli'd, and touch'd my trembling ears—   (70–77)

Not only do these lines prefigure the narrative program of Wordsworth's abortive venture, but Milton's "trembling ears" vibrate to the same shock waves as the "trembling hands" (subsequently revised to "trembling oars") with which the boy turns his boat around and thus faces away from the shape that pursues him, while submissively exposing his back to it.

The dynamics of Oedipal conflict remain the dynamics of Oedipal conflict whether they are played out in the precincts of the family or in the loftier arenas of literary history, and my purpose in calling attention to the latter dimension of the boat-stealing episode is not, by an irreversible interpretative strategy, to tease out from Wordsworth's childhood recollection the subtext of a more titanic cultural drama (though one wonders whether in

English cultural history the vesting of the figure of the poet with sublime patriarchal authority does not begin with Milton and end with Wordsworth). But neither am I suggesting that the literary drama is simply one more displaced enactment of a blocked script. For one can just as plausibly argue that the details of the childhood narrative are anachronistically conditioned by the adult poet's concerns as that those concerns are the precipitates of childhood experience, and one can find warrant for doing so in Wordsworth himself. Toward the end of book 1 of *The Prelude*, for example, the poet rather casually acknowledges, "I began / My story early, feeling, as I fear, / The weakness of a human love, for days / Disowned by memory—ere the birth of spring / Planting my snowdrops among winter snows" (640–44). This acknowledgment refers most directly to the lines in which Wordsworth "recalls" how the River Derwent "loved / To blend his murmurs with my nurse's song." But its avuncular accommodation of "days disowned by memory" is a useful, if disconcertingly candid, reminder that autobiographical accounts involve both a projection backward of the history a writer needs to create and the transcription forward of events inscribed in memory.

As I noted earlier, this is a familiar enough theme in autobiographical studies, but de Man's work has posed the problem of the referential status of the autobiographical text in ways that move beyond personal psychology to a consideration of what he describes, specifically in the context of speaking about Wordsworth, as a necessary interference between the thematic and rhetorical functions of language (*Romanticism and Contemporary Criticism*, 200n) or, in later formulations, between the tropological and performative functions of rhetoric. The conflicts de Man seeks to diagnose are, properly speaking, linguistic and philosophical rather than psychological, since they involve the mutually disruptive interdependency of two conceptual fields rather than the more or less ambivalent interaction of two conflicting tendencies, each with its own coherence and exigencies. Yet his identification of the focus of analytical labor as the place of interference between language as representation and language as performative positing has an evident affinity with Freud's account of conscience as the tangled nexus of internalized external authority and implacable drives "turned inward." Indeed, de Man himself invites such a comparison, albeit by negation, when in the "Excuses" essay, so much of which concerns language as a guilt-producing machine, he entertains the possibility that "the entire construction of drives, substitutions, repressions, and representations is the aberrant, metaphorical correlative of the absolute randomness of language, prior to any meaning or figuration" (*Allegories of Reading*, 299). What makes the boat-stealing passage

especially interesting and complex in this context is that the childhood recollection onto which Wordsworth projects backward his poetic ambitions is
itself, as we will see, a narrative about projecting backward.

J. Douglas Kneale has remarked in passing that "the back and forth imag-
inistic movement of *The Prelude,* its simultaneously progressive and retrospective temporality" is "emblematized in the boy rowing the boat, who
combines forward motion with retrograde vision" (*Monumental Writing,*
45). And Theresa Kelley has offered a careful analysis of how the methods by
which the child maintains his bearings in his surroundings move from
topology to projective geometry, according to a sequence for which she finds
broader developmental implications in Piaget (*Wordsworth's Revisionary
Aesthetics,* 54–55). Neither, however, considers the specific ways the narrative may function for Wordsworth as a disruptive mise-en-abyme of his autobiographical project. The reading that follows, then, seeks to address more
explicitly how perceptual, affective, and rhetorical mechanisms of projecting backward at play in the passage interact with one another. Given the
complexities of this articulation, I first look briefly at the woodcock-snaring
episode, an earlier, shorter and simpler sequence that can be seen as something of a dry run for the later passage. More specifically, the elaborate perceptual trap and its repercussions that loom so large in the boat-stealing
episode are largely absent from the earlier passage, so that a comparison may
bring out the differences the perceptual dimension makes.

LET ME BEGIN by noting some of the numerous points of similarity between the two episodes. In both Wordsworth recounts venturing out as a
child in a moonlit, uninhabited place. In both he comes upon something
bound to the spot by another's toil—in the one case the shepherd's tethered
skiff, in the other case a woodcock caught in another trapper's "toils." Each
time he takes the thing in secrecy, and each time, in the wake of his act, he
has an altered and uncanny apprehension of his surroundings and feels pursued by a monitory and retributive presence. Finally—and this is a point I
will come back to—since both stories pivot around an interdicted "act of
stealth" that but for Wordsworth's "telling" on himself would leave no trace
for others of its occurrence, they also bring into momentary play a confessional economy in which the poet's admission of wrongdoing functions as a
delayed restitution, returning to the domain of social representation and exchange a knowledge that the writer held as a secret possession.

Yet though both passages may be seen to traverse such a confessional moment, in neither case is the focal event of the story the revealed act itself;

rather, it is the uncanny apprehension it precipitates. And to the extent that the focus of the story shifts from the deed to its uncanny aftermath, the confessional economy it mobilizes is also being displaced. What happens in these passages is not a discharging of guilt but an exploration of its phenomenology and, via that phenomenology, of the borderlands of consciousness.

Within the narrative sequence of book 1 of *The Prelude*, the woodcock-snaring episode is the first recollection relating to the period following Wordsworth's mother's death and his subsequent "transplanting" (309) from his birthplace, Cockermouth, to grammar school at Hawkeshead. It thus implicitly occurs with the context of a separation from the family sphere and initiation into a social and economic[8] organization of wider range, an initiation that includes a socialization of and to male aggressive pursuits, in which craft and art figure as a means of dominating and appropriating nature. Thus, though the child is really trapping, in imagination he becomes a kind of pirate on the moors:

> In thought and wish
> That time, my shoulders all with springes hung,
> I was a fell destroyer. On the heights
> Scudding away from snare to snare, I plied
> My anxious visitation, hurrying on,
> Still hurrying, hurrying onward.   316–21[9]

The transgressions or "crossings over" here are multiple, involving a young child's assumption of adult pursuits ("on the heights," at night, alone, in an unguarded place), the human trespass against a nature that is transcendently other ("—moon and stars / Were shining o'er my head. I was alone, / And seemed to be a trouble to the peace / That was among them") and, as will emerge, the theft of property. Thus when in the wake of "the deed" the child feels himself pursued ("I heard among the solitary hills / Low breathings coming after me" [329–30]), we are clearly dealing with a peripeteia in which hunter and hunted exchange roles or, to recall Nietzsche's phrase, "the instinct of aggression is turned back upon itself." But again, what matters to Wordsworth is not simply that the child's passions are "directed back toward the place from which they came" (Freud), whether we understand that place as the child himself or the home he set out from, but that they are reflected back to him via the mediation of the surrounding landscape. Thus the vertical axis that opposes his "anxious visitation" to the transcendent peace of the heavens is now supplanted by an earthbound axis

of imaginative projection, along which first the hills and then the turf trans-
mit back to the child in a dissociated and ghostly form, scarcely differentiated from the landscape itself, the sounds generated by his own flight.
And it is of course precisely this "commutation and transfer of internal feelings, co-operating with external accidents" that, for Wordsworth, endows the
incident with its poetic significance.[10]

I REFERRED to the woodcock-snaring episode as a "dry run" for the boat-
stealing episode, in part, I must admit, because its "scudding away" (318)
takes place on land rather than water, but mainly because it rehearses a
movement whose steps the later passage recapitulates and carries further.
Structurally, that further stage corresponds to the narrative coda whose separation from the scene of what Wordsworth calls "the spectacle" is marked
by the relinquishing of the boat and its return to its mooring (whereas in the
earlier passage the fleeing child makes off with the goods and in virtue of
that possession remains identified with the object of predatory desire). It is
also marked by his movement away from not just the epicenter—let us call
it the first turning point—of the theft, but from the entire scene within
which the actions and their reversals have unfolded. Simply put, if this were
a play, the dramatization of the aftermath would require a change of set. In
fact, one would have to keep changing the set, for not only is the figure of the
pensive child's movement set against a different background ("There, in her
mooring-place, I left my bark, / And through the meadows homeward went,
with grave / And serious thoughts" [415–17]), but the ground itself keeps
shifting as we move from meadows to home to sleep and finally to the psychic space of dreams.

One could argue that the figure of the haunted child mediates between
the initial spectral threat and the poet's retrospective articulation of its experience: something is left behind ("There, in her mooring-place, I left my
bark") but something is also taken away ("And through the meadows homeward went, with grave / And serious thoughts)." And clearly one function of
the coda is to provide Wordsworth with a means of figuring the inward turn
to memory that for him is virtually constitutive of the possibility of poetic
utterance. But the relation between the "spectacle" and its recurrence in
memory does not correspond very well in this passage to a movement from
outer to inner, because the event or process Wordsworth refers to as "seeing
that spectacle" already involves a profound disturbance of the usual perceptual boundaries between outer and inner. Correspondingly, what haunts the
child cannot be understood as the reflection in memory of an external ob-

ject. *That* possibility is represented here by the privative reference to "no familiar shapes / Of hourly objects, images of trees, / Of sea or sky, no colours of green fields," (422–24) whose presence "in [his] thoughts" had functioned as guarantor, in their temporary absence, of the continuing existence of the things they represent. But it is that dimension of memory that is blotted out by the "darkness" in the child's thoughts, a darkness that stalks the sanctuary of inwardness as relentlessly as the spectral shape had invaded the solitude of the mountain lake. Thus when Wordsworth writes

> . . . and after I had seen
> That spectacle, for many days my brain
> Worked with a dim and undetermined sense
> Of unknown modes of being . . .   (417–20)

the ambiguity of the verb "worked," with its active and passive valences, registers the persistence in memory not only of the nameless, faceless shape but of the child's struggle to work free of it, a struggle that continues to make itself felt in the indeterminacy of the poet's language as it seeks to find words for an experience that ultimately it can only reinduce with, in Neil Hertz's phrase, "the pathos of uncertain agency" ("More Lurid Figures," 6).

I noted before that the way memory may be said to repeat the spectral event at the same time that it seeks to master it in representation is in part a function of the peculiar boundary-disturbing nature of that event. Let us turn now to the factors conditioning that disturbance. The child's initial discovery of the boat is situated within a narrative context that both relates it to and differentiates it from the opening of the woodcock-snaring episode. His ramble into the countryside is part of a succession of displacements to ever less familiar places of dwelling: having initially been transplanted from his birthplace to school and Hawkeshead, he now is on vacation from Hawkeshead, and lodged in the village inn in Patterdale, "a vale / Wherein I was a stranger" (375–76). His discovery of the boat is thus framed as an antipodal scene of maximal displacement and symbolic condensation—again, as Hertz would say, following Kenneth Burke, an end of the line scene (*End of the Line,* 218).

"Tied / Within a rocky cave, its usual home" (374–75), it presents the child with a proleptic, inanimate, and estranged image of himself tethered to a home that is a tomblike natural shelter mirroring antithetically the place of birth and the maternal body from which he has been progressively separated. Yet the shepherd's skiff itself is also one further place of residing in the home-school-inn sequence, with this difference: like any vehicle of self-transport, it is a mobile home, with reference to which the body is in relative repose though it is itself in motion. The wording of the 1850 text, "Straight I un-loosed her chain, and stepping in / Pushed from the shore," is particularly concise in registering the dynamic of reversal that the child's appropriation thus enacts: his occupancy, which places him within the boat as the boat was "at home" within the cave, is simultaneously a displacement of the boat from that "usual home." Narratively and psychologically, we move with this gesture into a looking-glass world in which the appearance of progression toward further self-differentiation conceals a regression toward stasis.

At this point it may be useful to briefly situate the analysis of the passage I am developing in relation to the Oedipal reading that Richard Onorato has clearly and influentially expounded. Onorato's interpretation depends on reading the boat-stealing scene as the displaced enactment, and its recollection therefore as the unconscious recollection, of a repressed scenario in which the absent owner of the boat is the father, the boat is the mother (as object of sensual gratification), and the child is a still younger incarnation of the poet who has not yet yielded, through identification, to the father's assertion of prohibitive authority. Here is a representative formulation: "When Wordsworth talks about 'stealth and troubled pleasure,' he is not really talking about stealing, which does not even describe accurately what the boy is doing. . . . It is rather the desire to possess momentarily, and to use to one's own passionate satisfaction, what belongs to another man that is the 'guilty' wish here. Psychologically, the appearance of the feeling of guilt should remind us of the formative causes of conscience" (*Character of the Poet*, 271).

Onorato's introduction of the Oedipal subtext turns then on whether Wordsworth is "really talking about stealing" and the guilt that colors the scene is proportionate to the actual transgression. We might rephrase Onorato's first point by saying that what is involved is what we would today call a "joyride" (a form of autoeroticism if ever there was one) rather than outright theft—call it stealing for keeps. But I would then further insist that connected with the desire for *temporary* enjoyment is the desire for *surreptitious* enjoyment, the desire that his act should leave no trace for others, not just of his identity, but of its having occurred at all (just as in the woodcock-snaring episode something is taken from another's keep without being missed). From the point of view of Onorato's reading, the function of stealth is primarily defensive: it provides cover for the enactment of a proscribed wish. What I wish to suggest, however, is that the desire to steal—in the intransitive sense of the verb—may be internal to the desire to steal in the transitive sense. (Note in this connection the recurrence of an intransitive "stealing" following the moment of traumatic confrontation: "With trembling hands I turned / And through the silent water stole my way." From this point of view, rather than the child's stealth functioning as a means by which he temporarily takes possession of an object, the object would be precisely a vehicle, a means by which he can indulge in an act of stealth and the "troubled pleasure" that accompanies it.)

This would imply a different subtext, one over which the Oedipal narrative would be overlaid, but also a different understanding of the writer's relation to the inward turn of autobiographical recollection. The concealment that envelops the theft involves a theft of knowledge in the sense that it seeks to lay claim to a knowledge to which the other is blind. As the sharing of that knowledge, the narrative has to refer to a sphere that is radically outside the space of representation—not to a particular piece of reality thus far unasserted, but to an event that disturbs the field of spatiotemporal representation. That is, the poet's narrative itself is set in motion at a critical point by a transgressive act of stealth vis-à-vis the reader. Specifically, the sentence "It was an act of stealth / And troubled pleasure" is rhetorically a self-authorizing gesture: in the absence of another witness, the admission of a transgression, the disclosure of something that would normally be concealed, functions as evidence of candor, but it also conceals its own rhetorical function in establishing authority by pretending to be something it cannot be: verifiable testimony. Thus the reference to an act of stealth and troubled pleasure that took place in the past simultaneously disguises a related stealthiness at work in the gesture of admission. The bad faith implicit in a gesture that denounces and sets at a distance an action very like the one it is performing is the flip side, as it were, of the evocativeness of the account, since the temporal distancing (it *was* an act of stealth) simultaneously marks a differentiation and sets up a pattern of correspondences.

Particularly in the 1805 version, which is not only religiously less orthodox but also less attentive to the virtues of narrative economy, the rhetorical interplay between differentiation and repetition makes itself felt in the way the sense of narrative development is countered by a regressive undertow that slows the action and verges on stasis. The conflicting tendencies are named in a simile that is, as I noted previously, a near repetition of lines from *Paradise Lost,* "my little boat moved on / Even like a man who moves with stately step / Though bent on speed." Indeed, and again this is conspicuously true only of the 1805 version, there is scarcely a narrative action or descriptive detail in this group of lines that is not itself either repeated or narrated twice. Thus, apart from such obvious examples of repetition as "I . . . struck the oars, and struck again / In cadence," the echoing of the oars' sound, or the symmetrical glitter of the wake, the action designated by "I unloosed her tether and embarked" is only minimally different from "from the shore / I pushed"; "my little boat moved on" is followed four lines later by "did my boat move on"; and the principal elements that compose the landscape— the moon, the mountains, and the reflective surface of the lake—are each named twice. That many of these features were edited out of the 1850 version, with virtually no loss of information or evocative power, is itself a good indicator of their structural redundancy.

One reason they are redundant is that there is a fundamental specularity to the represented scene, since what the child primarily apprehends are traces he leaves behind as he withdraws from the shoreline. It is not simply the boat that the child is withdrawing, but himself as his activity becomes gradually converted into the production of a spectacle of which he is the sole witness and as a succession of states gets gathered into the simultaneity of a picture.

Thus, rather than a clearly defined figure of action set against a ground (cf. "Straight I unloosed her chain, and stepping in / Pushed from the shore"), the "I" withdraws into a point of view that is structured as a movement of self-withdrawal. The body's active power tends toward automatism, while the child's backward gaze, the narrator's retrospective picture, and the reader's imaginative investment of the text tend to align in a single aestheticizing calm.

Coming immediately after the admission "It was an act of stealth / And troubled pleasure," the double negative assertion, "Nor without the voice / Of mountain-echoes did my boat move on," suggests that the child projects his own feelings of guilt as a monitory and unseen presence in the hills and relates the mood of this opening scene of withdrawal and projection to the conclusion of the woodcock-snaring episode. But whereas in the latter case there is no sound, only affective projection or the child's disassociated apprehension of his own movement and breath, here the monitory projection is mediated by an actual perception, whose object, however, is itself the repercussion within his surroundings of a sound originating in the child's activity, so that already there is a complex interplay between affective and perceptual structures of projection. The image that immediately follows, "Leaving behind her still on either side / Small circles glittering idly in the moon," sustains the complex structure of projection and cause-effect inversion, but the shift from sound to sight also shifts the trouble-pleasure gradient in the direction of the latter. To be more specific: on the one hand, the reflective circles the child propagates are, like the echoes, literally the lingering by-products of his activity as the stroke of the oars repeatedly roils the moonlit surface of the lake. But if we compare the image of "small circles glittering idly in the moon" to the related lines in the woodcock-snaring episode ("Moon and stars / were shining o'er my head; I was alone / And seemed to be a trouble to the peace / That was among them"), we can see that the child's "troubling" of the moonlit surface is immediately organized into the generation of a more complicated visual pattern that reflects back to him and thus sustains his own sense of idle sensual enjoyment.

The specular relation between the guilt of a transgressive act and the concealment of that guilt, which sets the story in motion, is in turned displaced by the second wave of the narrative: "And now, as suited one who proudly rowed / With his best skill . . . " At this point the ambivalence that colors the opening scene is surmounted, and we enter into something like the position of Oedipal identification. The resistance of the shore that propels motion and is recapitulated with each movement of the oars is now supplanted by a different structure that moves toward integration, and the affective disidentifications are replaced by a more purely cognitive mechanism, a feedback system that places seeing in the service of the efficient production of movement.

Given this pattern of development, whose successive phases may be said to be "driven" by the internal contradictions of a subject constituted by a movement of difference and negation and that sustains itself through compounded and ever-renewed negations of its relation to the object from which it differentiates itself, the phantasmagoric climax of the passage may seem like a thinly veiled encounter of the subject with the apocalyptic autonomy of its own imaginative powers: an anticipatory, but also evaded, encounter with the "mighty form" of imagination that later directly raises itself up, in book 6, before the "eye and progress" of the poet's song. Something of this interpretative tendency, for example, informs David Collings's conclusion that if Wordsworth had not actually undergone an experience like the one he recalls "he would have had to invent one" (*Wordsworthian Errancies,* 137) and Onorato's previously cited description of the scene as the "unconscious recollection of a climax of sexual fantasies." In either case, the basic spring of the projection would be an unconscious drive for mastery pressing for expression. The movement of projective reversal would express itself particularly in the striding movement of the peak that, in contrast with its apparent rising up, which could be accounted for in purely optical terms, would be the index of a psychologically motivated projection. But without entering into a detailed analysis of the perceptual mechanisms at work, I would argue that all the details of Wordsworth's description at this point can be accounted for in perceptual terms, that is, in terms of an aberration produced by the same mechanisms of projection that organize the feedback system in terms of which the child's visual and kinesthetic fields are integrated.

Simply put, there is a conflict between the kinesthetic and visual information the child is receiving, a conflict that opens up a space of perceptual aberration and reflects the contingency of their alignment. Rather than a conflict between what is perceived and what is projected, there is a disarticulation of two mechanisms of perception, a breakdown of eye-hand coordination. From this point of view the anthropomorphizing tendency of the passage, as it attributes voluntary power and intentional focus to the grim shape, is in fact a defensive projection against fragmentation that is itself, in the present narrative, only contingently articulated within the moment of perceptual breakdown. One may speculate that affect systems in general arise at points of rupture in cognitive systems—that these furnish, as it were, the "stuff" of affect—and therefore that they cannot strictly speaking be represented, since they are disturbances within representational systems, whether we are speaking of perception, memory, or language in its cognitive capacity. But this does not amount to a *conflict* between affect and cognition; rather it constitutes an articulation between affect and cognition at those points where the coherence, or one might say, the workability of a cognitive structure reveals its contingency.

It may well be, then, that investigations into the relation between mechanical perceptual models and affectively motivated mechanisms of projection may also provide us with a way of thinking about the relation between the representational and rhetorical dimensions of language and that Wordsworth's narrative is, among other things, such an investigation.

The Autobiographical Object

Patterns of Incorporation in Rousseau and Wordsworth

Thus the shadow of the object fell upon the ego.
—SIGMUND FREUD, "Mourning and Melancholia"

*W*e are accustomed to speaking of the "I" of autobiographical writing as "the autobiographical subject." The "object" at issue in the title of this chapter is the one whose shadow, in Freud's memorable phrase, falls upon the ego, *das Ich*, the "I," i.e., eclipses it.

A story Freud reports in the chapter on identification in *Group Psychology and the Analysis of the Ego* (1921) summons up this shadowy object: "A child who was unhappy over the loss of a kitten declared straight out that now he himself was the kitten, and accordingly crawled about on all fours, would not eat at table, etc." (*Standard Edition*, 18:109). Freud cites this example to illustrate how "identification with an object that is renounced or lost, as a substitute for that object—introjection of it into the ego . . . may sometimes be directly observed in small children."[1] Preceded by a consideration of "the genesis of male homosexuality in a large class of cases" (108) and followed by a discussion of melancholia, both being in Freud's reading less transparent manifestations of the same phenomenon, the example does indeed have the virtue of literally speaking for itself, since the child not only acts like the lost kitten but verbally identifies himself with it. The child's "straight out" declaration, which both designates and extends into the realm of speech the wish-fulfilling trajectory of an otherwise nonverbal performance, permits Freud to momentarily ground his own claims about identificatory incorporations in an open and spontaneous (albeit aberrant) pronouncement by the object of his analysis.

Although in "Mourning and Melancholia" (1917) Freud had treated the pattern exemplified by this anecdote as pathological—the "healthy" response to object loss being to get oneself a new object—by the time he wrote *The Ego and the Id* (1923) he had come to view it as so "common" and "typical" as to constitute perhaps "the sole condition under which the id can give up its objects" (*Standard Edition*, 19:28–29). Yet one may legitimately ask whether, even as its explanatory range is extended, Freud's simple schema does not harbor unanalyzed complexities, which have continued to bedevil psychoanalytic theory. As anyone can attest who has looked into the psychoanalytic literature on the "four *Is*"—incorporation, introjection, identification, and internalization—there does indeed seem to be, in Diana Fuss's summary formulation, "a difficulty . . . in identifying identification" (*Identification Papers*, 4).

Something of this latent complexity may be noted in the example we began with, for it is less transparent than it first appears. On the one hand, if the child "acts out" his identification with the lost object, this performance requires that the parents serve as its audience, taking over the subject position the child had formerly assumed. Let us suppose what seems implicit in this scenario, that the kitten was a "transitional object," by means of and in relation to which the child had taken his distance on an earlier developmental phase. Then his ways of playing kitten—crawling on all fours, not eating at table, etc.—would also signal regression to an infantile, preverbal relation to his parents.

On the other hand, the child's identification involves a withdrawal from others into the reflexive, self-absorbed, and consuming activity of making *himself* feel he is the kitten, a withdrawal marked especially in his refusal to eat at the family table. From this point of view, the child's declaration might well serve to hide the fact that the kitten is missing and missing *because* the child has taken it into himself.

In any case, the example's apparent transparency belies—and one begins to suspect it may be a function of—the implicit complexity of the context from which it is removed. Similarly, the distinctness of the psychoanalytic formula it supports, "identification with an object that is renounced or lost, as a substitute for that object," may not so much conceal as neatly condense into a manageable *topic* a more diffuse and clouded area of inquiry. In *Identification Papers*, Diana Fuss argues that the distinction between object choice and identification, "which together," in her account, "form the cornerstone of Freud's theory of sexual identity formation" (11), cannot itself be stably established, an argument that has predictably met with resistance from more orthodox—and one cannot help but feel ostentatiously heterosexual—quarters.[2] Without wading too deeply into the details of this argument, we may recall Freud's allowance in *The Ego and the Id* that "at the very beginning, in the individual's primitive oral phase, object-cathexis and identification are no doubt indistinguishable from one another" (*Standard Edition,* 19:29). In terms of the debate between Fuss and her critics, this and similar acknowledgments by Freud cut both ways. For her part Fuss can say, "Even Freud is unable to keep desire and identification completely straight" ("Look Who's Talking," 391). For their part her critics can argue that Freud's theory is aware of and accommodates the difficulty that Fuss portrays as the Achilles' heel of his swollen foot: "Freud does in fact insist that identification and object choice are indistinguishable at the root, that is, in the preoedipal stage of development." What concerns us rather is that in this passage Freud associates the conceptual indistinction Fuss insists on specifically with "the oral phase."

Supposing this is so, why should this quandary be relevant to an understanding of Romanticism? And more specifically, why should it be relevant to a consideration of the understanding of Romanticism as a mode of internalization? An answer may be derived from the example we began with and the play between the "object of desire" and the "object of address" around which its drama of incorporative identification turns. Generalizing, I suggest that Freud's notion of identification with the lost object involves both a "taking in" and an "acting out," but that the relation between these two dimensions of the problem—between, so to speak, Freud's pictures of inhibition and pictures of exhibition—is by no means clear, since the ambivalence of narcissistic identification encompasses my relation to the other not only as object of desiring memory but also as potential audience or interlocutor. At the same time, this complication points up the potential usefulness of Freud's approach for thinking about Romantic autobiography, since it also characterizes the rudimentary structure of Romantic autobiographical testimony. For as we saw in our introductory examination of Rousseau's preamble to his *Confessions,* the Romantic autobiographer's identificatory relationship with an interiorized memory is inextricably bound up with the text's testamentary relation to its future readers.

To what extent, then, do the dynamics of what Freud speaks of as "regression from object-cathexis to narcissistic identification" have something to tell us about such autobiographical discourse? And to what extent do the dynamics of this discourse have something to tell us about the psychoanalytic schema? The pages that follow explore these questions through the reading of two particularly paradigmatic autobiographical texts from the Romantic period.

I TAKE my first example from Rousseau's posthumously published *Confessions,* specifically the inaugural paragraphs of book 6. Most of book 6 deals with his sojourn at Les Charmettes, a rented country property, with Mme de Warens, the aristocratic benefactress and lover whom Rousseau famously refers to as "Maman," his actual mother having died in giving birth to him. Rousseau begins the book by declaring that the brief period of happiness he is about to recall has given him "le droit de dire que j'ai vécu" [the right to say I have lived], the right, we might say, to publish his *Confessions.* And he then goes on to claim for his *memories* of the period a comparable status:

> Rien de tout ce qui m'est arrivé durant cette époque chérie, rien de ce que j'ai fait dit et pensé tout le tems qu'elle a duré n'est échappé de ma mémoire. Les tems qui précédent et qui suivent me reviennent par intervalles. Je me les rappelle inégalement et confusément; mais je me rappelle celui-là comme s'il duroit encore.

> [Nothing that happened to me during this cherished time, nothing that I did, said, or thought all the time it lasted, has slipped from my memory. The times preceding it and following it come back to me at intervals; I recall them irregularly and confusedly; but I recall that time as if it still existed.] (*Oeuvres complètes,* 1:226)

The vividness and plenitude of these memories stand out from the lesser power of other memories. Their strength in the domain of representation derives directly from a prior preeminence in the domain of lived experience. In the sentences that immediately follow, however, Rousseau offers a much more complicated accounting of his autobiographical undertaking, one that invites comparison with Freud's story of regression from object cathexis to narcissistic identification:

> Mon imagination, qui dans ma jeunesse alloit toujours en avant et maintenant rétrograde, compense par ces doux souvenirs l'espoir que j'ai pour jamais perdu. Je ne vois plus rien dans l'avenir qui me tente; les seuls retours du passé peuvent me flatter, et ces retours si vifs et si

vrais dans l'époque dont je parle me font souvent vivre heureux malgré mes malheurs.

[My imagination, which in my youth always looked forward but now looks back, compensates me with these sweet memories for the hope I have lost forever. I no longer see anything in the future to attract me; only a return into the past can please me, and these vivid and precise returns into the period of which I am speaking often give me moments of happiness in spite of my misfortunes.] (1:226)

The way Rousseau talks about autobiographical recollection in this latter passage is much closer in its emphases to Freud's story of regression from object cathexis to narcissistic identification. The pleasure Rousseau finds in recollection—and it is the pleasure rather than the truthfulness of memories that is now at stake—depends on the prior occurrence of a period of happiness with a companion that can now be recalled: "cette époque chérie." But it depends equally on the possibility of its recurrence having been lost forever, "pour jamais perdu," at the same time that it is rediscovered in memory: "Ces retours si vifs et si vrais dans l'époque dont je parle me font souvent vivre heureux malgré mes malheurs."

Following these general remarks, Rousseau tells a story to illustrate how vividly everything that happened to him during his stay at Les Charmettes with Mme de Warens impressed itself on his memory. And he demonstrates the power and accuracy of these memories not simply by recalling in detail an episode from the period, but also by recalling a later occasion when his memory of that time made itself felt. As we will see, however, in establishing his epistemological authority to speak from memory, Rousseau ends up enacting in a particularly detailed and telling manner the pattern Freud describes.

Je donnerai de ces souvenirs un seul éxemple qui pourra faire juger de leur force et de leur vérité. Le prémier jour que nous allames coucher aux Charmettes, Maman était en chaise à porteurs, et je la suivois à pied. Le chemin monte, elle étoit assez pesante, et craignant de trop fatiguer ses porteurs, elle voulut descendre à peu près a moitié chemin pour faire le reste à pied. En marchant elle vit quelque chose de bleu dans la haye et me dit: voila de la pervenche encore en fleur. Je n'avois jamais vû de la pervenche, je ne me baissai pas pour l'examiner, et j'ai la vue trop courte pour distinguer à terre les plantes de ma hauteur. Je jettai seulement en passant un coup d'oeil sur celle-là, et près de trente ans se sont passés sans que j'aye revû de la pervenche, ou que j'y aye fait attention. En 1764 étant à Cressier avec mon ami M. du Peyrou, nous montions une petite montagne au sommet de laquelle il a un joli salon qu'il appelle avec raison Belle-vue. Je commençais alors d'herboriser un peu. En montant et regardant parmi les buissons je pousse un cri de joye: *ah voila de la pervenche;* et c'en était en effet. Du Peyrou s'apperçût du transport, mais il en ignoroit la cause; il l'apprendra, je l'espére, lorsqu'un jour il lira ceci. Le lecteur peut juger par l'impression d'un si petit objet de celle que m'ont fait tous ceux qui se rapportent à la même époque.

[I will offer a single example of these memories that will allow one to judge their force and truth. The first day that we set out to spend the night at Les Charmettes, Maman was in a sedan chair, and I followed her on foot. The path climbs, she was fairly heavy, and worrying that she would tire out her porters, she wished to get down midway along and complete the journey on foot. In walking, she saw something blue in the hedge and said to me, "Here's some periwinkle still in flower." I had never seen any periwinkle, I didn't bend down to look at it, and I am too shortsighted to distinguish from a standing position plants on the ground. I simply tossed a glance at this one in passing, and more than thirty years passed without my having seen periwinkle again, or having noted that I did. In 1764, while I was staying with my friend du Peyrou at Cressier, he and I climbed a little mountain at the summit of which he has a pretty pavilion he rightly calls Belle-vue. At that time I was starting to botanize a little. In climbing and looking among the bushes, I called out in joy: *ah, here's some periwinkle;* and so it was. Du Peyrou observed my transport, but he was ignorant of its cause. He will learn it, I hope, when one day he reads this. By the impression of so small an object, the reader may judge that made on me by all those that relate to the same period.] (1:226)

"One recalls the episode of the periwinkle," writes George Poulet, discussing affective memory in Rousseau. "The flower Rousseau sees reminds him of the same flower noticed in his youth when he was coming home to Charmettes, and the impression of so small an object suffices to place him once more in the state of mind of those former years" (*Studies in Human Time,* 179). Yet what strikes one in reading this passage is precisely that it describes the original moment of perception as in fact less vivid than its repetition years later. Indeed, Rousseau emphasizes in a number of ways that he scarcely pays any attention at all to what Mme de Warens points out: he neither stoops nor pauses to look, giving the flower only a glance (and a nearsighted one at that) as he walks by. Everything contributes to reducing the image of the periwinkle to a blur, "quelque chose de bleu dans la haye." Then, by contrast, each of these deficiencies is corrected in the later episode. Where before Rousseau had declined to stoop, he is now "looking among the bushes." The passing and silent glance has now become an arresting moment of recognition and exclamation. And in place of the reference to his nearsightedness ("la vue trop courte"), Rousseau now notes that he and his companion du Peyrou were on their way to "a pretty pavilion he rightly calls Belle-vue," that is, lovely sight. Rather than resurrecting in all its freshness a past moment of experience, Rousseau's joyful sighting of the periwinkle adds to the original perception a vitality and precision—"force et vérité"— it lacked.

A "straight up" deconstructive reading of the passage might at this point ask whether the text does not in fact produce the chain of experiences from which it claims to derive and whether Rousseau does not expose the fictive dimension of his *Confessions* in the very process of seeking to demonstrate their truth. But before going this route, I propose a slightly different tack, one that will at least temporarily bring us back to Freud, as I suggested in introducing this passage. For the discrepancy between the two moments is best understood when we consider that Rousseau reenacts not so much his own experience as that of Mme de Warens, since it is after all her gesture and utterance he repeats. A structure of displaced repetition governs the relation between virtually all features of the two scenes. Thus Rousseau's rummaging among the bushes, marked in the text as a kind of stooping, further identifies him with Mme de Warens, who had condescended to climb down from her sedan chair. And his own earlier role as the uncomprehending witness of her delight devolves on the friend du Peyrou, who like Rousseau will appreciate later what he did not at the time.

In seeking to establish by this exemplary story his "droit de dire que j'ai vécu," Rousseau thus retraces the pattern of incorporation Freud was to delineate in "Mourning and Melancholia." And indeed, what separates the two moments of the his story is not only thirty years but the death of "Maman": for Mme de Warens died in July 1762 and Rousseau's visit with du Peyrou took place in the fall of 1764, thus shortly before he began work on the *Con-*

fessions. But if Freud's account of regression from object cathexis to narcissistic identification as a response to loss offers us a model for understanding
the structure and function of autobiographical recollection in Rousseau,
Rousseau's text also allows us to situate the object of Freud's insight within
a broader context.

If it is true, for example, that Rousseau fails to find a replacement for "Maman," and thus that the cry "ah voila de la pervenche" is effectively addressed
to himself, nonetheless the self-savoring quality of the moment is qualified
by the anticipation of du Peyrou's deferred participation in Rousseau's pleasure. In this regard it is worth noting that Rousseau expresses the "hope" that
in reading the *Confessions* du Peyrou will come to understand Rousseau's delight, since this seemingly casual gesture of acknowledgment counterpoints
Rousseau's preceding assertion that hope is something he has "lost forever."

The doubleness of du Peyrou's role, first as uncomprehending witness
and then as sympathetic reader, is of course tied to the fact that the object of
our analysis is a written text rather than a purely inward process of recollection. Up until now I have obscured this point by conflating in my exposition
the scene of writing and the scene of recollection. For du Peyrou can participate in Rousseau's pleasure only on condition of having been originally ex-
cluded from it: had Rousseau explained to him at the time the reason for his
exclamation, du Peyrou would not have understood or felt it in the same way.
The intimacy between them is made possible only by the delay and distance
embodied in the encrypted text, since a similar delay and distance are fundamentally constitutive of Rousseau's experience in the first place. Paradoxically, the communicative power of the passage depends on a prior narcissistic moment that suspends communication. In fact, multiplying delays
organize du Peyrou's relation to the episode and underlie his anticipated
identification with Rousseau. First, as just seen, the possibility of his "learn-
ing the cause" of Rousseau's transport depends on the delaying of an explanation. Second, it depends on that explanation's being received in Rousseau's
absence, that is to say, only after its deposition in written form. Finally,
Rousseau stipulates that the seal on this deposition is to be broken by du Peyrou, to whom he entrusted the manuscript of the first half of his *Confessions*
for safekeeping and for eventual publication only after his death.

The periwinkle episode shows us that Freud's account of melancholia as
regressive identification does not end there. It is part of a longer chain of
identifications, reversals, and displacements that eventuates in what Paul de
Man described as "the autobiographical moment": "an alignment between
the two subjects involved in the process of reading in which they determine

each other by mutual reflexive substitution" (*Rhetoric of Romanticism*, 70). And at least in the example we are considering, the beginning and end points of this series of displacements also seem to be clearly gendered. The movement from origin to end, from speech to writing, from presence to absence, is also a movement from the domain of the mother, "Maman," to that of the father, du père, du Peyrou.[3] But if in Lacanian terms the story seems to record and enact a movement from the imaginary to the symbolic, a relinquishment of the maternal object and submission to the paternal law of substitution, it would be more accurate to say that it performs a continual displacement of that turn.

Although the reading of the passage I have been elaborating is a critical one in that it focuses on discrepancies between what Rousseau says he is doing in telling his story and what he shows himself to be doing, it is also what I would call a "friendly" reading, in the sense that it does not seriously question Rousseau's version of events or seek to undo the charm and poignancy of the episode. The text I have been reading is, as I have noted, a text destined for a friend, and if I have more or less unwittingly put myself in the position of du Peyrou, the faithful editor and friend, I suppose this is to solicit the benign attention of my own readers. But one ought to be at least somewhat suspicious of a text that manages simultaneously to advertise its narcissism and make exceptional claims for its referential authority, all the while cultivating a decorous intimacy of exchange with its readers.

Giving play to that suspicion would involve examining more closely the role assigned to "Maman" both in Rousseau's text and in my reading of that text. Although I have argued that, as regards Rousseau's own conduct in the two moments of the story, it may be difficult to distinguish sharply between a prior moment of object cathexis and a later moment of narcissistic identification, there seems to be no ambiguity as far as Mme de Warens herself is concerned. For she, in contrast to Rousseau, is attentive to everyone and everything around her and uses language to name what is at hand and to address Rousseau in his presence. One would need to consider how the vivacity of her gesture depends for its meaningfulness on the contrast it forms with the elevation and repose to which her social and sexual status consign her. One would also need to consider the way the whole story hinges on her having a past that Rousseau does not share, of which the periwinkle is the token. Finally, one would need to consider the patterns of identification, patterns no longer predominantly intersubjective, that link both Mme de Warens and du Peyrou with the periwinkle, unexpectedly "still in flower."

Since such an extended reading demands a consideration of the episode's larger narrative context, I turn instead to another text that more explicitly uses figures of mourning to dramatize identifications of a less intersubjective and gendered character. Like Rousseau's story of the periwinkle, Wordsworth's well-known lines on the Boy of Winander divide into two scenes, the second involving a commemoration in secret of the first. Again, but this time explicitly, not simply a lapse of time but a death divides the two scenes. And again, a complex structure of identifications bridges the discontinuity marked by death. I cite from the 1805 version of *The Prelude:*

There was a boy—ye knew him well, ye cliffs
And islands of Winander—many a time
At evening, when the stars had just begun
To move along the edges of the hills,
Rising or setting, would he stand alone
Beneath the trees or by the glimmering lake,
And there, with fingers interwoven, both hands
Pressed closely palm to palm, and to his mouth
Uplifted, he as through an instrument
Blew mimic hootings to the silent owls,
That they might answer him; and they would shout
Across the wat'ry vale, and shout again,
Responsive to his call, with quivering peals
And long halloos, and screams, and echoes loud,
Redoubled and redoubled—concourse wild
Of mirth and jocund din. And when it chanced
That pauses of deep silence mocked his skill,
Then sometimes, in that silence while he hung
Listening, a gentle shock of mild surprize
Has carried far into his heart the voice
Of mountain torrents; or the visible scene
Would enter unawares into his mind
With all its solemn imagery, its rocks,
Its woods, and that uncertain heaven, received
Into the bosom of the steady lake.

This Boy was taken from his mates, and died
In childhood ere he was full ten years old.
Fair are the woods, and beauteous is the spot,
The vale where he was born; the churchyard hangs
Upon a slope above the village school,

And there, along that bank, when I have passed
At evening, I believe that oftentimes
A full half-hour together I have stood
Mute, looking at the grave in which he lies.   (5.389–422)

In speaking of a bridging structure of identifications, I refer first to the way the apostrophe to the landscape with which Wordsworth interrupts or calls out across the narrative almost as soon as it has begun ("There was a boy—ye knew him well, ye cliffs / And islands of Winander—") invites comparison with the boy's own "mimic hootings to the silent owls, / That they might answer him." But I am also thinking of how the poet's spells of mute absorption ("oftentimes, / A full half-hour together I have stood / Mute, looking at the grave in which he lies") repeat and further deepen the "pauses of deep silence" (in another version, "lengthened pause of silence") within which the boy's still expectancy merges with the abiding stillness of the landscape:

And when it chanced
That pauses of deep silence mocked his skill,
Then sometimes, in that silence while he hung
Listening . . .

I will return later to the opening apostrophe. For the moment I want to elaborate on the identificatory connections between the coda and the narrative preceding it. It is not just that the adult's silence resonates with the child's or that, as has been frequently noted, the phrase "the churchyard hangs" echoes "while he hung / Listening." For the circumstances composing the churchyard tableau, "along that bank when I have passed / At evening . . . oftentime / . . . I have stood mute," condense the haunted twilights of the opening with the ensuing silence.

—many a time
At evening, when the earliest stars began
To move along the edges of the hills,
Rising or setting, would he stand alone
Beneath the trees or by the glimmering lake . . .

Such recurring recurrence to an appointed place at an appointed moment—the keeping, one might say, of an appointment with disappointment—confers on the later scene its own sense of phantasmal rendezvous.

If I am right that the coda records or enacts a moment of identificatory embodiment, the specific quality of that embodiment may be clarified by comparison with another of Wordsworth's poetic codas. In a footnote to the preface to the *Poems of 1815,* Wordsworth offers the following comment on "There was a boy": "Guided by one of my own primary consciousnesses, I have represented a commutation and transfer of internal feelings, cooperating with external accidents, to plant, for immortality, images of sound and sight, in the celestial soil of the Imagination" (*Selected Poems and Prefaces,* 487n). The language of this comment may equally remind us of the final stanza of "Daffodils":

> For oft when on my couch I lie
> In vacant or in pensive mood
> They flash upon that inward eye
> Which is the bliss of solitude,
> And then my heart with pleasure fills,
> And dances with the daffodils.

This coda, like that of "There was a boy," frames a moment of incorporative identification—here one in which the poet's reclining body (no more a wandering "cloud that floats on high"), merges with the remembered landscape, both flower bed and brimming lake. Lest this reading seem unduly fanciful, consider the following extract from Dorothy Wordsworth's *Grasmere Journals* written on 29 April 1802, two weeks after the entry that was to serve William as a source for his poem:

> We then went to John's Grove, sat a while at first. Afterward William lay and I lay in the trench under the fence—he with his eyes shut and listening to the waterfalls and the birds. There was no one waterfall above another—it was a sound of waters in the air, the voice of the air. William heard me breathing and rustling now and then, but we both lay still and unseen by one another. He thought that it would be as sweet thus to lie in the grave, to hear the peaceful sounds of the earth and just to know that one's dear friends were near. (117)

In "Daffodils," the shift from narrative to coda entails only the absence of the remembered, valued object and can thus be adequately dramatized as a shift from what happens "outside" to what happens "inside." "There was a boy," by contrast, entails the loss of the subject as well. Not only have "images of sound and sight" been "planted for immortality in the celestial soil of the imagination," but the earth now holds the body of the boy himself.

In contrast to the other poem, then, the division between narrative and coda in "There was a boy" marks a gap in the subjective continuity of the poem, leaving the narrator's relation to the narrated scene uncanny and unaccounted for. The break does not simply mark the passage of an unspecified amount of time but itself occurs as a moment of structural anomaly (a shifting from the conventions of omniscient to first-person narration), in its effect not unlike the grammatical anomaly we encounter a few lines before: "a gentle shock of mild surprize / *Has* carried far into his heart" (my emphasis).

We can, of course, call on any number of explanations to mend this rift, including the likelihood, well supported by manuscript evidence, that Wordsworth is recalling experiences from his own childhood. For "There was a boy" trails a complex and ambivalent textual history. One of the very earliest parts of *The Prelude* to have been composed, it appears first in a notebook from 1798–99, between two versions of what was to become the boat-stealing episode of book 1. In this well-known manuscript version, the boy is the poet himself. Wordsworth then recast these lines entirely in the third person, added the graveside coda, and included the piece in the 1800 edition of *Lyrical Ballads*, making it one of a very few parts of *The Prelude* to have been published during his lifetime. Later the piece occupied a prominent place in the *Poems of 1815*, and in the preface to this volume, in the note I referred to earlier, Wordsworth speaks of the poem as "guided by one of my own primary consciousnesses," thus broadly hinting at its autobiographical basis. Typically, Wordsworth later deleted this note.

As should be evident, the textual history raises as many questions as it lays to rest. On the one hand, the evidence of the early variant for the identification of poet and boy dovetails so neatly with consecrated strategies for reading Romantic poetry (and especially Wordsworth's) as a poetry of more or less veiled self-reflexivity that even readers who normally eschew any appeal to the authority of origins find it hard to resist the temptation to play this philological ace in the hole. On the other hand, once the autobiographical subtext is restored, it becomes hard to understand why Wordsworth should have chosen to shroud it. The decision, curious in itself, is doubly so when the poem is returned to its context in *The Prelude*, where, according to Wordsworth's argument, the episode is supposed to illustrate the way nature educates the child to a "knowledge not purchased by loss of power."

In his commentary on the poem in *Wordsworth's Poetry*, Geoffrey Hartman deals with this difficulty by emphasizing how the coda "injects a new emphasis on inwardness. The strange half-hour pause suggests that he looks

not only at something external, a grave, but also at something within, his former heart . . . the survivor contemplates his own buried childhood" (21). In
the Gauss lectures he delivered not long after Hartman's book had appeared,
de Man, without explicitly referring to Hartman at this particular point, rejects this reading with his dismissive epithet of choice: "It would be banal
and inadequate to say that Wordsworth is praising and mourning in the
poem his own youth, the boy he used to be" (*Romanticism and Contemporary Criticism*, 81). Now, if such a reading is indeed "banal," that banality is
surely there in Wordsworth's writing and not simply in Hartman's reading.
Indeed, it seems to me that de Man at this time made Hartman's reading the
repository of this banality in order not to have to deal with it in Wordsworth
(something he later sought to do).[4] Hartman, for his part, implicitly acknowledges that banality, explaining the introduction of the boy's death as
a literalizing concession "to the prevalent taste . . . [a] conventionalizing incident" (20). The "strange half-hour pause" that ensues restores at once the
inwardness and the figurality of the narrative. For as we saw, Hartman reads
the passage as the substituting of something external—the boy's body in the
grave—for something "within—Wordsworth's former heart," and this is
also the substitution of a literal understanding for a figurative one, a movement the autobiographical reading then reverses.

But a slightly different reading of the graveyard scene is possible, one in
which figuration and interiorization are not two sides of the same coin. Certainly Wordsworth's revision of the early manuscript turns into the figural
narration of the loss of a former mode of object relation that is now preserved in melancholic self-communing, but it is also true that his rewriting
actively encrypts or buries the earlier version of the poem within the later
one. From this point of view, the grave is a figure for the material text, and
its temporal structure is metaleptic: the poem commemorates as an event
preceding it a burial it in fact performs. By the same token, the graveside
scene offers an anticipatory emblem for Wordsworth's relation to *The Prelude* as a whole, since he withheld the text from publication but returned to
it for revision throughout his life.[5]

Ultimately, though, the interpretation I am proposing need not call on
the poem's compositional history at all. For along with the narrative rift, the
mere linguistic gesture by which the poet withholds the child's name ("There
was a boy—ye knew him well, ye cliffs / And islands of Winander—") in itself constitutes a cryptic bond of identity between poet, child, and landscape.
That is to say, it functions comparably to the suppression of the first person,

executing an elision that is then narrated as the taking of the boy "from his mates."

In short, what we read as a psychological development that the narrative records may also be read as an action the poem is performing on a set of linguistic counters. This possibility does not invalidate an autobiographical reading of the poem, but it suggests that both such a reading and the development it traces depend on the suppression of discontinuities of a fundamentally linguistic nature. (This suggestion warrants comparison with Otto Kernberg's hypothesis that psychic development depends on the substitution of repression for splitting as a mechanism of defense.) The phantasmal, guilty, ambivalent element of identificatory processes—the loved object is missing because I have incorporated it—is the carrier of this linguistic event, and in "There was a boy" we can see the obsessive repetition of a series of identificatory embodiments moving toward its disclosure.

In a sense it matters little whether we imagine that the unspoken name of the apostrophe is someone else's or that it is Wordsworth's own, or indeed that there is no name—that the grave is empty—and that that is what is unspoken. All these unavoidable speculations are ways of trying to make sense of the excessive and repetitive element in Wordsworth's language, of the way the very literalness—call it banality—of its expression makes his self-dramatizing something close to a lie, a mock or mimic mourning: "the grave in which he lies."

‘Five

Action, Internalization, and Utterance

Structure and Gender in the Romantic Lyric

$\mathcal{T}$hus far I have focused on the nature and function of internalization in the processes by which Romantic writing sought to differentiate itself from the scriptural legacies to which it was heir and by which two writers in particular, Wordsworth and Rousseau, sought to stake their claims of originality and authenticity. Questions of gender and sexuality have perforce surfaced in the course of these inquiries, but they have not been thematized as such. In this chapter I introduce these questions more explicitly, first of all by examining another poetic narrative by Wordsworth that is organized around the recollection of a boyhood exploit, the lines titled "Nutting." Originally intended by Wordsworth as part of the "poem on my own life," "Nutting" has a close structural affinity with the boat-stealing episode and offers a remarkably clear demonstration of how far the strategies of internalization we have been considering, along with the tensions they harbored, were inscribed within an ongoing, if increasingly ambivalent, male project of self-representation.[1]

Although most of the argument that follows will emerge through a close reading of "Nutting," the contours of that reading are shaped by a historical hypothesis that should be made explicit, since it may seem questionable for a variety of reasons. More specifically, I assume that the possibility of claiming public identity as a lyric poet—which is not the same thing as writing lyric poetry—remained an essentially male prerogative well into the nineteenth century, even as women were increasingly contesting recognition as writers. Although such a claim no doubt requires substantiation and qualification (one of Wordsworth's earliest poems was, after all, a tribute to the poet Helen Maria Williams), it is, I think, an implicit corollary of the generally acknowledged fact that in the industrial West the fortunes of women writers as a class were tied to the fortunes of the novel.[2]

I also propose that, for the same reasons that the figure of the lyric poet was emphatically marked out as a male, the male lyric poet's involvement with language was haunted by a correspondingly drastic threat of feminization. If writing novels was potentially identifiable as "women's work," it nonetheless remained a form of marketable labor, whose productivity and value could be measured in concrete economic terms. Writing poetry, by contrast, might seem an all or nothing proposition, either an act of imaginative sovereignty that by definition transcended questions of audience or economic reward and thus offered an image of male social autonomy in its sublime form (think of Wordsworth's justly famous remark that "a great poet must create the taste by which he is to be enjoyed") or else something abjectly nonproductive.

Like the boat-stealing episode, "Nutting" revolves around the poet's recollection of a childhood act of transgressive appropriation, in this case the violent plundering of a secluded hazel bower. And like the boat-stealing episode, the poem was originally supposed to figure in *The Prelude* as an example of the "ministry" by which nature shaped the poet's imagination. Eventually, however, it was "struck out as not being wanted there" and published with some modifications in the 1800 edition of *Lyrical Ballads*. One can only speculate, of course, about Wordsworth's reasons for this decision, but may he not have isolated the passage because it fit in all too well and raised too explicitly sexual issues that he was prepared to acknowledge but just as glad not to enshrine in the official biography?

The sexual loading of the narrative begins with the poem's title and at times approaches transparency, as when Wordsworth's refers to the secluded bower as a "virgin scene" or speaks of himself as gazing upon it "with wise restraint voluptuous." At a more unconscious level, the child is also described as comically encumbered by phallic accoutrements, "a huge wallet o'er [his] shoulder slung / A nutting-crook in hand" while "sallying forth" "in the eagerness of boyish hope." A subsequent description of the bower and the trophy it harbors ("the hazels rose / Tall and erect, with tempting clusters hung") suggests that the "virgin scene" is also a phallicized female body. Although these latter lines give some sense of just how complexly overdetermined the imagery of the poem may be, they also confirm the basic and more or less avowed symbolism of the exploit: in plundering the bower, the boy seeks, as through a violent act of sexual depredation, to lay claim to his manhood.

But what is the connection between the symbolic drama the child enacts and the symbolic activity of the adult poet in recalling this drama? On the one hand, Wordsworth is clearly conscious of the sexual violence implicit in the incident and specifically distances himself from it. He depicts his childhood self with considerable irony, as we have seen, and the lesson of tenderness with which the poem concludes ("Then, dearest Maiden, move along these shades / In gentleness of heart; with gentle hand / Touch—for there is a spirit in the woods") is clearly meant to contrast, both in tone and in substance, with the child's violent assertions of masculinity. Thus it is possible for Uri Knoepflmacher, in writing about gender integration in Wordsworth, Eliot, and Woolf, to cite "Nutting," with some justification, as an example of how "Wordsworth deliberately subverts a destructive masculine fancy" and of how, "by depreciating that lesser fancy, the ironic male speaker subordinates himself to the superior sororal imagination of . . . that 'dearest Maiden' invoked at the end of [the poem]" ("Genre and the Integration of Gender," 98–99). In this reading, the poem clearly functions as a compensatory offering.

On the other hand, the recollected incident continues to be valued *by the adult* as a rite of passage initiating the child into a privileged imaginative relationship with nature and thereby preparing him for his vocation as a poet. This interpretation of the incident is more or less explicit in the earlier version of the poem intended for *The Prelude* and is in any case implied by the narrative structure of the passage. Moreover, and this is the point that will especially concern us, the writing of the poem itself functions as a confirming reenactment of this initiation. That is to say, the process of recollection is structured in the same way as the child's acts and partakes of a related violence.

We may observe that, despite the tender ruefulness of the poem's concluding lines, the narrative opens in an exhilarated flourish of identification:

> ————It seems a day
> (I speak of one from many singled out)
> One of those heavenly days that cannot die.

Placed at the threshold of the poem, these opening lines, with their thematic and grammatical suspension of chronology, orient the ensuing narrative, from the start, toward a moment of climactic recollection. The ironic stance Wordsworth adopts in the lines immediately following, and by which he seems to underscore the temporal and emotional distance separating him from his childhood self, thus in fact links the poet with the child who "in the eagerness of boyish hope, / . . . left [the] cottage-threshold . . . / . . . and turned [his] steps / Tow'rd some far-distant wood . . . / Tricked out in proud disguise." To formulate the point in somewhat schematic terms: the child stands in relation to the "far-distant wood" as the poet stands in relation to the affectively and temporally distanced memory he intends to evoke. One could follow in detail the ways the recollected incident is thus shadowed by the process of its recollection, drawing out, for example, the connections between the poet's conspicuous deferral of narrative closure and the "wise restraint voluptuous" with which the child delays harvesting his prize. But what concerns us most directly here is the culminating moment of this process:

> . . . unless I now
> Confound my present feelings with the past;
> Ere from the mutilated bower I turned
> Exulting, rich beyond the wealth of kings,
> I felt a sense of pain when I beheld
> The silent trees, and saw the intruding sky.

We may note, first, the breakdown of temporal boundaries signaled by the poet's interjection and, second, the disruptive potential of the suggestion that the adult may be wishfully projecting backward a feeling he claims to recollect. This confusion of identities between recollecting and recollected selves functions in part as the structural counterpart of the child's ravaging of the bower, the ecstatic present heralded by the poem's opening lines and toward which the entire narrative has advanced.

One may object that what the poet is repeating in this moment is precisely not the boy's willful violation but rather his sense of sympathetic identification with the landscape. From this point of view the poet's openness to past feeling, his uncertainty about where in time to locate the source of that "sense of pain" (In the adult or in the child?), is linked to the child's uncertainty about where to locate it in space (In himself or in the woods?). And to judge by the poem's last line, it is on behalf of this feminine "spirit" of sympathetic identification that the poem is spoken and in this spirit that Wordsworth asks that the poem be read. Such a tranquil sense of communion can be sustained, however, only if we choose to forget the poet's hesitancy in attributing sympathetic feeling to the child and, furthermore, to overlook the elements of projection and appropriation that such a movement of sympathy would in any case imply. For the child's sense of pain not only depends on an act of violence but is itself an act of imaginative violence. It projects onto the landscape a human sense of passive and suffering muteness in order that the child may then incorporate in himself, in the slow moment when he mutely gazes on the scene, the "quiet being" that the bower has "patiently given up."

What is happening in this moment cannot, I acknowledge, finally be understood as either violent or tender, active or passive. What Wordsworth speaks of here as "a sense of pain" is itself an agitated uncertainty about the boundaries of the ego, an agitation that disturbs the stability of such oppositions as well as the opposition between male and female in terms of which the poem organizes its thematic statement. Similarly, the uncertainty the poet experiences in narrating this moment is not quite the same thing as an act of pure projection, though I have been stressing the projective aspect in my reading.

Nevertheless the narrative pattern of the poem as a whole, with its progressive intensifications and condensations, works to locate and confine, and thereby limit, the effects of this ambivalence. And to the extent that the poem's central ambivalences are resolved and that the meaning of the experience can be stated, the social identity of the speaker is confirmed. In particular, the *turn* from recollective narrative to exhortation in the poem's closing lines ("then, dearest Maiden, move among these shades / In gentleness of heart; with gentle hand touch . . .") should be seen as reenacting the gesture by which the child turns from the mutilated bower, "Exulting, rich beyond the wealth of kings." It is not so much the ambivalent moment of recollection as it is this voice of ethical instruction that is the poet's harvest.

With this movement from recollection to exhortation, questions of gender again become explicit. For what is most disconcerting about this conclusion is that it is addressed to that "dearest Maiden," Dorothy. Where did she come from and what has she done—or might she do—that *she* should be the object of this admonition? Knoepflmacher's suggestion, quoted earlier, that the speaker "subordinates himself to the superior sororal imagination" leaves no way of accounting for why it is the maiden who is being instructed here and not the poet. I would suggest, on the contrary, that the appearance of this maidenly figure at the end of the poem underscores the speaker's maleness at the moment that the public and ethical significance of his utterance is being confirmed. To state the matter in somewhat different terms, the reassertion of gender differences reinforces the more problematic distinction between the poet's utterance and the child's action, which is why the maiden is made to take the place of the guilty child at the same time as she is set over against the poet.[3]

Although a partial reading of one poem is obviously no basis for generalization, "Nutting" offers a fair example, I believe, of the way questions of poetic identity and questions of sexual identity impinge on one another in Romantic poetry. The social task the Romantic poets found themselves historically assigned was a self-contradictory one, that of giving public, linguistic embodiment to a self that was by definition private and inward. Their language registers the pressure of that contradiction without resolving it, and to that extent it resists ideological appropriation, though it also resists understanding. At the same time, however, the movement from action to internalization to utterance that "Nutting" enacts and that is characteristic of Romantic poetry attempts to portray this contradiction as a dialectical interaction between a masculine will and a feminine experience of interiority, with poetic utterance figuring as the mode of action of an internalized self. What I have sought to point out is that regardless of how the poet defined his position in this conflict, the project of self-representation remained defined as a male prerogative and responsibility, in ways the poet could do little to control.

The Stewed Muse of Prose

Wordsworth, De Quincey, and Baudelaire

> The illustrious poets, annoyed by the platitude of prose, speedily
> relinquished their uncongenial task.
>   —MARY SHELLEY, "Author's Introduction" to *Frankenstein*

*I*t is a "wet, ungenial summer" in Switzerland; everyone has been
reading ghost stories to pass the time, and now Byron, in his play-
ful, peremptory way, has proposed that each of you write one. If in this situation you find that your story is not coming along, it is apparently one of
the advantages of being an illustrious poet—or more precisely of being two
illustrious poets—that you can agree to blame your difficulties on "the platitude of prose," at which point the weather will suddenly clear and you can
head off together for the mountains. But should you happen to be the wife
of one of these poets and under his constant urging to "enrol [your]self on
the page of fame," you may find yourself doubly immobilized, chained to the
task of writing by your very inability to perform it. Thus Mary Shelley:

> I thought and pondered—vainly. I felt that blank incapability of in-
> vention which is the greatest misery of authorship, when dull Nothing
> replies to our anxious invocations. "Have you thought of a story?" I
> was asked each morning, and each morning I was forced to reply with
> a mortifying negative. (*Frankenstein*, 58)

At the furthest possible remove from illustrious poets and the page of
fame, what Shelley dramatizes at this moment in her account of the circum-

stances attending the conception of *Frankenstein* is precisely her consign-
ment to the "platitude of prose," both as the inmost zone of her subjection
to the obliterative pressure of circumstance and as the site of her resistance
to that pressure. For the same indefinite sense of limitation that the poets
consign to the "platitude of prose," she absorbs and concentrates in herself
as a "blank incapability of invention." But she also personifies it as "dull
Nothing [replying] to our anxious invocations" and finally animates it in the
figure of the monster who stands at its creator's bedside, "opening his cur-
tains and looking on him with yellow, watery, but speculative eyes" (59).

If Shelley's subjection to her husband's literary tutelage thus embodies the
subordination of prose to poetry within a received hierarchy of literary
value, this relationship, I would argue, is neither adventitious nor simply a
matter of analogy. Rather, it is graphic evidence that with the entry of
women into an expanding literary marketplace during the eighteenth century, the distinction between poetry and prose became charged with the
function not only of underwriting the autonomy of the poetic text vis-à-vis
the value-determining power of the commodity system but also and correlatively of shoring up the poet's representative privilege as, in Wordsworth's
phrase, "a man speaking to men."[1]

In light of this claim, in this chapter I analyze a sequence of nineteenth-
century texts by three male writers whose work worries the distinction between poetry and prose. More particularly I argue, through examining one
of Baudelaire's prose poems, "La Soupe et les nuages," that the subversion in
his later work of the hierarchical distinction between poetry and prose is
bound up with a subversion of gender hierarchies and that both processes
are linked to the foregrounding of a metaphoric of oral incorporation. Since
Baudelaire is not usually accused of harboring a feminist agenda, he may
seem like an odd candidate to enlist in the service of such a project. But his
reputation for misogyny is partly what makes him an interesting figure in
this context, for it suggests that the transformative processes—at once textual and social—that are under way in this work override personal attitude.

To know the genre of a work is to possess a foreunderstanding that can,
to a considerable extent, guide critical analysis, not because it prescribes interpretations but because it shapes the questions one poses. Precisely because of its generic indeterminacy, the task of reading "La Soupe et les nuages," as with all of Baudelaire's prose poems, is immediately dependent
on—is continuous with—the broader task of discovering or inventing the
kind of reading it will respond to. In part then because of the difficulty and
strangeness of the piece, I approach it obliquely and in stages, by first exam-

ining some more familiar texts with which it invites comparison—one by Wordsworth, another by De Quincey. Although the textual sequence I will be unfolding also retraces a genealogical chain, I should make it clear that the genealogical claims are *ancillary* to the main thrust of the argument.

THE CLOUDS of "La Soupe et les nuages" appear to have drifted across the channel from the mountainous retreats of Wordsworth's *Excursion,* where in book 2 the Poet accompanies his "revered Friend," the Wanderer, on a journey to visit the Wanderer's somewhat less revered friend, the Solitary. As they travel, the Wanderer details the misfortunes and disappointments that led the Solitary to "[fix] his home . . . / Among these rugged hills" (307–9), and both assume the worst when they see from afar a burial procession setting off from the single cottage in the vale. The Solitary himself, however, soon appears to explain that the funeral is for another inmate of the cottage, an old man on parish relief, whose story he in turn relates. The housewife whom the parish paid for the old man's keep (and from whom the Solitary rents his lodgings) had sent him out, despite threatening weather, to gather fuel on the moors, where he was overtaken by a storm; the next day a search party found him there, dazed and soon to die, among the roofless ruins of a small chapel. As they bore him home through the mist, the Solitary trailed behind, till a chance step freed him from "the skirts / Of the blind vapour" (830–31):

> The appearance, instantaneously disclosed,
> Was of a mighty city—boldly say
> A wilderness of building, sinking far
> And self-withdrawn into a boundless depth,
> Far sinking into splendour—without end!
> Fabric it seemed of diamond and of gold,
> With alabaster domes, and silver spires,
> And blazing terrace upon terrace, high
> Uplifted; here, serene pavilions bright,
> In avenues disposed; there, towers begirt
> With battlements that on their restless fronts
> Bore stars—illumination of all gems!
> By earthly nature had the effect been wrought
> Upon the dark materials of the storm
> Now pacified: on them, and on the coves,
> And mountain-steeps and summits, whereunto

The vapours had receded,—taking there
Their station under a cerulean sky.   (834–51)

In their immediate context these lines—obviously enough a naturaliza-
tion of the topos of the heavenly city, as the continuation of the Solitary's
speech will make explicit—stand in hyperbolic contrast to the preceding description of the old man's decrepit refuge on the heath. They thus dramatize
the Solitary's identification with the old man's victimized condition, an
identification inseparable from the anger and resentment he vents at their
landlady, sarcastically referred to as "our dame, the queen / Of this one cottage and this lonely dale" (775–76).[2]

The poet's own investment in this speech, and the scene in which it is embedded, is ambivalent. On the one hand, we are clearly meant to view with
irony the effusions of a speaker who, we are told, is "Steeped in a self-in-
dulging spleen that wants not / Its own voluptuousness" (311–12). On the
other hand, the passage bears an obvious resemblance to such signature
landscapes as the Snowdon episode of *The Prelude*[3] or "Composed upon
Westminster Bridge." Moreover, in a well-known passage from his preface to
The Excursion, Wordsworth compares the envisioned totality of his poetic
production to a complex hierarchy of architectural forms, likening *The
Recluse* to the body of a Gothic church, *The Prelude* to its antechapel, and his
minor pieces to "the little cells, oratories, and sepulchral recesses, ordinarily
included in those edifices." Based on this latter passage especially, I would argue that the lines from *The Excursion* we are examining envision the elevation of their own language, or more precisely the elevation of the poet's language to the rank of sacred authority.

The self-reflexive dimension of the passage is even more apparent when
we consider its position within the structure of narrative entailments that
organizes book 2 of *The Excursion* as a whole: the Poet tells us about the Wanderer, who tells the Poet about the Solitary, who tells both Poet and Wanderer about the dead man for whom he has been mistaken. Dead men, of
course, tell no tales, nor, in the interval between his rescue and his death,
does the doomed man testify to his ordeal other than by a "silent change."
But it is precisely in place of the dead man's tale that we are given this piece
of rhapsodic description. The mobile architecture of the clouds is thus
framed as a climactic displacement or vacating of the narrative function, an
end of the line projection of the transcendence of narrative temporality.[4]

This movement of self-transcendence is marked in specific figures, such
as that of "blazing terrace upon terrace, / high uplifted" or the self-coronat-

ing image of "towers begirt / With battlements that on their restless fronts / Bore stars—illumination of all gems!" Moreover, as the passage builds toward its climax in the lines immediately following these, it at first explicitly *compares* the grandiose forms of the scene to "Such as by Hebrew Prophets were beheld / In vision" (867–68)[5] and finally yields to a moment of enraptured identification:

> This little Vale, a dwelling-place of Man,
> Lay low beneath my feet; 'twas visible—
> I saw not, but I felt that it was there.
> That which I *saw* was the revealed abode
> Of Spirits in beatitude: my heart
> Swelled in my breast.—"I have been dead," I cried
> "And now I live! Oh! Wherefore *do* I live?"
> And with that pang I prayed to be no more!—
> —But I forget our Charge, as utterly
> I then forgot him.   (870–79)

With these lines, the speaker enacts a double identification: his vision identifies him with the dead man, but his speaking identifies him with the prophets and his language with the language of revelation. Indeed, what the closing remark ("—But I forget our Charge, as utterly / I then forgot him") implies is that the power exerted on him by his own language and the power of the vision are one: in each case time and the body of the dead man are forgotten. The opening description prefigures the speech's subsequent movement, via a poetic language of semblance and appearance (of which the clouds are the figure), toward this moment of prophetic identification. The figure of the old man is introduced and then sacrificed so that the text can enact its passage from an aesthetic to a sacred order, while the figure of the housewife functions as a repository of the blame that is needed for the pathos of his victimization.[6]

THE LINES from *The Excursion* we have been examining are cited anonymously by De Quincey in *Confessions of an English Opium Eater*—the book's only extended citation of poetry. The citation occurs in the section titled "The Pains of Opium," just after a famous passage on the mises-en-abyme of Piranesi's dream prisons and is introduced by the following remarks:

> With the same power of endless growth and self-reproduction did my
> architecture proceed in dreams. In the early stage of my malady, the

splendours of my dreams were indeed chiefly architectural: and I beheld such pomp of cities and palaces as was never yet beheld by the waking eye, unless in the clouds. From a great modern poet I cite part of a passage which describes, as an appearance actually beheld in the clouds, what in many of its circumstances I saw frequently in sleep. (106)

Note that in lifting these lines out of their dramatic context De Quincey instinctively disregards the problematic mediating role of the Solitary: the passage is offered, directly and without qualification, as the description by "a great modern poet" of "an appearance actually beheld in the clouds." This is reasonable enough, since the speech is, after all, in verse and therefore, as we have noted, in some sense must be the utterance of a poet. But De Quincey is also clearly anxious to invoke the figure of the Poet, rather than that of the Solitary, as an authorizing model for his own representational project. Like Freud, De Quincey presents his autobiographical book of dreams as a medical treatise. But this essentially prosaic discourse can aspire to the status of a work of art even if it cannot sustain that status, and the thought of Wordsworth's poetic voice bearing witness to De Quincey's experience figures the realization of that aspiration. Just as the poet, in a curious formulation, is said to have "actually beheld in the clouds" what De Quincey has seen frequently, but only "in sleep," so Wordsworth's autobiographical poetry authenticates the aesthetic potential of De Quincey's prose. In short, De Quincey's identification of "a great modern poet" as the adequate subject of his experience is akin to, but displaces, the Solitary's unstable identification with the figure of the prophet. To state the matter somewhat differently, Wordsworth's poetry here stands in relation to De Quincey's prose as the language of prophecy stands to the poetic text De Quincey cites.

The direction of the identification can always be reversed, however, so that De Quincey's prose becomes the medium in which the figure of the poet is contaminated by association with the figure of the opium eater, in the same way that the verse of *The Excursion* is a medium in which the figure of the prophet is contaminated by association with the figure of the Solitary. Thus Wordsworth must have been less than wholly pleased to find his poetry cited to illustrate the effects of opium eating, and as a matter of fact De Quincey originally declined to name the "great modern poet" to whom he was paying homage, because of concern for Wordsworth's at the time "imperfectly established" reputation.[7]

The pattern of reversal is particularly clear in the paragraph immediately following the citation:

> The sublime circumstance—"battlements that on their restless fronts bore stars,"—might have been copied from my architectural dreams, for it often occurred.—We hear it reported of Dryden, and of Fuseli in modern times, that they thought proper to eat raw meat for the sake of obtaining splendid dreams: how much better for such a purpose to have eaten opium, which yet I do not remember that any poet is recorded to have done, except the dramatist Shadwell: and in ancient days, Homer is, I think, rightly reputed to have known the virtues of opium. (107)

A heightened moment of appreciation ("The sublime circumstance—'battlements that on their restless fronts bore stars'") leads directly to the thought that the poet could have been "copying" De Quincey just as De Quincey has, quite literally, been copying the poet. The notation of this inversion is then followed by the hearsay report that Dryden and Fuseli "thought proper to eat raw meat for the sake of obtaining splendid dreams," a suggestion that further assimilates the figure of the poet to that of the opium eater while appropriately muddying the truth status of De Quincey's prose. And the self-corroborating assertion that "Homer is rightly reputed to have known the virtues of opium" (For who is the authority to whom that "rightly" appeals, other than De Quincey himself?) brings the process of inversion to a triumphant conclusion, with its celebratory play on the pharmacological and moral meanings of "virtue."

Let us now focus on one detail of this edifying sequence: De Quincey's rapid descent from the "sublime circumstances" of Wordsworth's verse to the "raw meat" of Dryden's and Fuseli's atavistic dietary practices. The violation of decorum achieved here is both thematic and stylistic: not only is the subject matter inappropriate but so, in their monosyllabic and unadorned literality, are the very words "raw meat." The result is paradoxical: precisely because of their extreme literality, the words "raw meat" become simultaneously a figure for what De Quincey's text ought not to, but does, include— for what De Quincey ought not to, but does, say, have in his mouth. The phrase thus restores and even intensifies the figurality of the diction it violates. Indeed, this brief sequence emblematizes the rhetorical structure of De Quincey's whole book—not to say his life—a structure wherein the literal, prosaic representation of a proscribed act of incorporation functions simultaneously as a figure for the violation of linguistic decorum it performs. De Quincey's opium eating becomes a figure for the prosaic incorporation of poetic elevation, not only by the appropriating citation of the poet's words but also, and in a more decisively condensed fashion, by the mere pronouncing of the poet's name.

ABOUT THE TIME the first edition of *Les Fleurs du mal* appeared and Baudelaire was beginning to think about the book of prose poems that was to appear posthumously as *Petits poèmes en prose* (and later as *Le Spleen de Paris*), he also began to work on a treatment—part translation, part condensation, part critical study—of De Quincey's *Confessions,* which was eventually published in 1860 as the second half of *Les Paradis artificiels* and that includes a rendering of our passage from "The Pains of Opium."[8]

> D'étonnantes et monstrueuses architectures se dressaient dans son cerveau, semblables à ces constructions mouvantes que l'oeil du poète aperçoit dans les nuages colorés par le soleil couchant. Mais bientôt à ces rêves de terrasses, de tours, de remparts, montant à des hauteurs inconnues et s'enfonçant dans d'immenses profondeurs, succédèrent des lacs et de vastes étendues d'eau. (1.482)

> [Stunning and monstrous architecture arose in his brain, resembling those moving constructions that the eye of the poet beholds in clouds colored by the setting sun. But soon these dreams of terraces, of towers, of ramparts, rising to unknown heights and sinking into immense depths, were followed by lakes and vast expanses of water.]

As an undeniable, albeit unconscious, point of textual contact between Baudelaire and Wordsworth, this excerpt from *Un Mangeur d'opium* exerts a certain fascination of its own. In the present context, however, I cite it only to point out that Baudelaire's prose poem, "La Soupe et les nuages" involves yet a further reworking of this material. Here then is the prose poem:

> La Soupe et les nuages
>   Ma petite folle bien-aimée me donnait à dîner, et par la fenêtre ouverte de la salle à manger je contemplais les mouvantes architectures que Dieu fait avec les vapeurs, les merveilleuses constructions de l'impalpable. Et je me disais, à travers ma contemplation: "—Toutes ces fantasmagories sont presque aussi belles que les yeux de ma belle bien-aimée, la petite folle monstrueuse aux yeux verts."

Et tout à coup je reçus un violent coup de poing dans le dos, et j'entendis une voix rauque et charmante, une voix hystérique et comme enrouée par l'eau-de-vie, la voix de ma chère petite bien-aimée, qui disait: "—Allez-vous bientôt manger votre soupe, sacré bougre de marchand de nuages?"[9]

[Soup and Clouds

My crazy little love was giving me dinner, and through the open window of the dining room I contemplated the moving architecture that God makes with vapors, the marvelous constructions of the impalpable. And I said to myself, through my contemplation, "All these phantasmagorias are almost as beautiful as the eyes of my beautiful love, the crazy little monster with green eyes."

And all at once I got hit by a violent punch in the back, and I heard a voice, raucous and charming, a hysterical voice, as though roughened by aqua vitae, the voice of my dear little love, who was saying, "Are you going to eat your soup soon, you holy bugger of a cloud monger?"]
(1.350)

Seeing that "La Soupe et les nuages" is informed by Baudelaire's translation of De Quincey's citation of Wordsworth can help us in understanding the prose poem in two respects. First, and at a fairly rudimentary level of interpretation, it makes it clearer that the daydreamer genially referred to by his companion as a "holy bugger of a cloud monger" is in more everyday language a poet. (In this respect it is worth noting that Baudelaire replaces De Quincey's specific, albeit anonymous, reference to "a great modern poet," with the generic label "l'oeil du poète," thereby reinforcing the emblematic status of the spectacle.)

Second, the pattern of rhetorical transformation we traced in De Quincey's writing can tell us something about the prose poem's reductive thrust and the figure it executes. At first reading it may seem that the relation between the two paragraphs of the prose poem, like that between the two nouns of the title—or for that matter between the two inhabitants of the household—is simply one of jarring incompatibility, both thematic and stylistic. Thus, for example, the elaborate loft and indeterminacy of "je contemplais les mouvantes architectures que Dieu fait avec les vapeurs, les merveilleuses constructions de l'impalpable"—all of this to say "I was looking at the clouds"—is literally flattened by the deadly precision of "Tout à coup, je reçus un violent coup de poing dans le dos," while the vapid and idealizing gallantry of "ma petite folle bien-aimée, ma belle bien-aimée," etc. (thinly

veiling, but nonetheless veiling, its undercurrent of aggression) is contra-
dicted, at every imaginable point, by the superbly vulgar ridicule of "sacré
bougre de marchand de nuages." As we saw with De Quincey, however, such
abruptly desublimating shifts of register, at the same time that they violate a
rhetorical code, will precipitate a reinscription of the violation they perform
within a condensed, metafigural narrative. In her path-breaking study of
Baudelaire's prose poetry, *Défigurations du langage poétique,* Barbara Johnson analyzes this effect in terms of a "conflict of codes": "This opposition between the figurative and the literal does not reduce to an opposition between
the symbolic and the real, for, precisely insofar as it is a sign of genre, the status of the act of 'eating' in a text, however literal it may be, is in fact always
symbolic, always makes up part of a code" (106).

Thus the prosaic "soup" of Baudelaire's second paragraph not only offers
an incongruous contrast to the poetic, figural "clouds" of the first but also
figures as the ultimate precipitate of a symbolic condensation channeled by
the downpour of "une voix hystérique et comme enrouée par l'eau-de-vie"
and heralded, as by a thunderbolt, by the sudden blow from behind. The tra-
ditional reading of "La Soupe et les nuages" as a comic dramatization of the
conflict between the ideal and the real[10] conceived as antithetical poles does
not address the insistence of this figural chain, though it is precisely this insistence that constitutes the text's challenge to interpretation.

But whereas De Quincey subverts this polarity by inscribing the figure of
the poet in a Swiftian physiological economy, within which the poet's body/
name functions as the locus of an exchange between the production of
"splendid visions" and the consumption of "raw meat," Baudelaire's text in-
scribes that figure in a market economy, specifically in the naming of the
poet as a "marchand de nuages" and more generally by recasting the act of
consumption itself as a form of alienated labor. Thus if "soupe" has here replaced "raw meat" as the figure of incorporable substance, that is at least in
part because the former embodies labor time. Furthermore, as succinctly in-
dicated by the poet's other oxymoronic epithet, "sacré bougre"—an epithet
that all but explicitly refers back to the violent blow from behind that sails
into the middle of this text[11]—Baudelaire's short course in home econom-
ics includes a frank unit on sex education, thus intuitively recovering the thematics of gender and social economy that formed part of the context of the
passage from *The Excursion* but was effectively occluded by De Quincey's appropriation of that passage. Somewhat less esoterically, the symbolic hierarchy invoked in the first paragraph clearly involves a hierarchy of gender as
well: on the one hand, God the creator, ethereal clouds, a sublime architec-

ture; on the other hand, a woman who is also a servant, supper, a dining room, with the male poet somewhere in between. His body may be at the dinner table, but his thoughts are absorbed in contemplation of the clouds. And he has time to "space out" because he is being waited on, in both senses of the phrase, by a woman: that is, his fantasy of transcendence or vacation of the moment imposes as its complement an embodied image of female servitude. In the context of this symbolic hierarchy the last sentence of the first paragraph ("Et je me disais, à travers ma contemplation: 'Toutes ces fantasmagories sont presque aussi belles que les yeux de ma belle bien-aimée, la petite folle monstrueuse aux yeux verts'") clearly functions as a self-admiring gesture of condescension, betokening the poet's sense of the power of his language to mediate between high and low, inner and outer, immaterial and material.

This movement of condescension is both disrupted and hyperbolically embodied by the opening of the second paragraph, for the subject of "tout à coup je reçus un violent coup de poing dans le dos" is not situated "between" the high and the low, but quite literally between "la folle bien-aimée," who is behind him, and his supper, which is on the table in front of him. No longer a figure of mediation along a vertical axis of transcendence, the *je* of the speaker is simply the vehicle of a transmitted impulse, expelled across a series of discontinuous moments. At the same time, however, the poet's vaporous thoughts and internalized speech, both tokens of a fantasy of mastery, are supplanted by the raucous voice of an intoxicated woman who both commands him and calls him names (thus the description of her voice structurally parallels the description of the clouds—to which it is further linked by the figure of "l'eau-de-vie"—while the final citing of her words parallels the previous moment of self-citation), so that the second scene inverts and displaces the hierarchical relationships of the first.

(Here a biographical note: there is evidence that the last sentence of the piece is a rough citation of words addressed to Baudelaire by a woman named Berthe with whom he was involved toward the end of his life. Her last name is not preserved in the Pléiade archival material. Some time after they had broken up, Baudelaire presented her with a montage in the shape of an inverted T.[12] The vertical axis divides into three sections. The top section is a drawing by Baudelaire of Berthe facing right—the good way. The middle section is a poem to her, titled "Les Yeux de Berthe" [cf. "les yeux de ma belle bien-aimée"]. The bottom section is another drawing of Berthe, but this time facing left—the bad way. This section is also the middle of the horizontal axis. To its left we find an embryonic version of "La Soupe et les nuages": "Comme, pendant le dîner, je regardais les nuages par la fenêtre ouverte, elle me dit: Allez-vous bientôt manger votre soupe, sacré marchand de nuages!" [As, during dinner, I was looking at the clouds through the open window, she said to me: Are you going to eat your soup soon, you holy cloud monger!]. To its right Baudelaire has inscribed a dedication: "à une horrible petite folle, Souvenir d'un grand fou qui cherchait une fille à adopter, et qui n'avait étudié ni le caractère de Berthe, ni la loi sur l'adoption. Bruxelles, 1864" [to a horrible little fool of a woman, a memento from a great fool of a man who was looking for a daughter to adopt, and who had studied neither Berthe's character nor the law on adoption. Brussels, 1864]. The structure of this montage should be compared with the structure of the prose poem.)

Another of Baudelaire's prose poems, "Les Tentations, ou Eros, Plutos, et la Gloire," evokes the mystery of a voice "dans laquelle je retrouvais le souvenir des contralti les plus délicieux et aussi un peu de l'enrouement des gosiers incessament lavés par l'eau-de-vie" [in which I recognized the memory of the most delicious contraltos and also something of the hoarseness of throats incessantly washed by aqua vitae]. The voice, it emerges, is that of the goddess of fame, who trumpets the poet's name throughout the universe. In "La Soupe et les nuages" as well it is a question of naming and recognition, but the goddess of fame, who elevates the poet's name, has become the stewed muse of prose, and the recognition she offers, to a figure as allegorical and as nonallegorical as herself, is of a very different kind: for the function of the physical blow is less to injure than to summon the other's attention, while the function of the name calling—the violence wrought, as in effigy, on the poet's name—is not at all to summon but to inflict an injury. The blow opens up a space within which her words then leave their mark, and it is this two-stage process of inscription—which is also the release and then rebinding of a violence in language and in sexuality—that the second paragraph transcribes.

The muse of prose is not inspiring and is therefore not a muse. We can say that what Baudelaire is doing with this Punch and Judy show is disfiguring both muse and poet, but we should recognize that the rhetorical violence implied by the term is not something his prose poetry inflicts from without on poetic language but is rather a violence latent in the idealization of poetic language that the prose poetry brings out. And if we say that Baudelaire was temperamentally suited for this task, we should also say that this temperament was inseparable from his lucidity about his craft. It is striking to me that this lucidity should have led him not only to see that the suppression of the prosaic dimension of poetry was related to the social oppression of women but to solicit—in his writing—the partial exorcism of both.

Seven

Drinking Rules!

Byron and Baudelaire

*P*ursuing the argument of the previous chapter, here I take up two nineteenth-century texts on the theme of intoxication[1] in which the poetic word is no longer able, if it ever was, to stably figure itself as the metaphoric other of the drug—that is, as a *legitimate* means of imaginative transport—and in which the writer's enthrallment by the transporting substance of words shows us its addictive and one might say prosaic face.

The first of these pieces is a pair of stanzas from the second canto of Byron's *Don Juan*, the other Baudelaire's brief prose poem "Enivrez-vous." That they may be connected was proposed first by Jean Pommier (*Dans les chemins de Baudelaire*, 341) and then, following Pommier, by Robert Kopp (Baudelaire, *Petits Poèmes en prose*, 314–15), though neither reader enters into much more detail than to note that both bits of writing, in Kopp's words, "chant[e] l'ivresse." The praise of drunkenness is of course a poetic commonplace, and the mere fact of its appearance in these two bits of text argues about as intimate a bond of kinship as that involved in pointing out that we are all Noah's children. But there are some more compelling reasons for looking at these pieces in relation to one another, and I believe Pommier was responding to them.

That Byron mattered to Baudelaire is attested by a number of references scattered throughout the latter's work and letters, references that, though faulting Byron for garrulousness, praise him for having the thing that makes poets: "une diabolique personnalité" (*Correspondance*, 2:232). Perhaps the most interesting of these references occurs in a well-known letter Baudelaire wrote to his mother in July 1857, shortly after *Les Fleurs du mal*

had been published and while the storm of controversy that was to culminate in the collection's prosecution and expurgation for obscenity was
rapidly gathering:

> On me refuse tout, l'esprit d'invention et même la connaissance de la
> langue française. Je me moque de tous ces imbéciles, et je sais que ce
> volume, avec ses qualités et ses défauts, fera son chemin dans la mé-
> moire du public lettré, à côté des meilleurs poésies de V. Hugo, de Th.
> Gautier et même de Byron.

> [They deny me everything, the spirit of invention and even knowledge
> of the French language. I could care less about all these imbeciles, and
> I know that this volume, with its qualities and its faults, will make its
> way in the memory of the lettered public, along with the best poetry
> of V. Hugo, of Th. Gautier, and even of Byron.] (*Correspondance*, 1:411)

The pride of place Baudelaire reserves for Byron in this list was somewhat
dated even in its time and is odd in other ways,[2] especially given the more
qualified expressions of admiration we meet elsewhere in his writings. But
it becomes more understandable if one considers that Baudelaire's mother
was of Byron's generation and had early ties to England (in fact, she apparently taught Charles English during his childhood [E. Crépet, 30],[3] making
it, strangely enough, part of his "mother tongue"). For her Byron's would
have been the emblematic case of a writer in whom a reputation for de-
pravity was overtaken by poetic honor, perhaps at the cost of his death in a
noble cause.

Apart from this evidence of a felt affinity, there are specific formal
grounds for associating the two pieces. Since they are fairly brief, I will quote
them both. Here are the stanzas from canto 2 of *Don Juan*:

179

Man, being reasonable, must get drunk;
    The best of life is but intoxication:
Glory, the grape, love, gold, in these are sunk
    The hopes of all men, and of every nation;
Without their sap, how branchless were the trunk
    Of life's strange tree, so fruitful on occasion:
But to return,—Get very drunk; and when
You wake with head-ache, you shall see what then.

180

Ring for your valet—bid him quickly bring
   Some hock and soda-water, then you'll know
A pleasure worthy Xerxes the great king;
   For not the blest sherbet, sublimed with snow,
Nor the first sparkle of the desert-spring,
   Nor Burgundy in all its sunset glow,
After long travel, ennui, love, or slaughter,
   Vie with that draught of hock and soda-water.

And here is Baudelaire's prose poem:

XXXIII
Enivrez-vous

   Il faut être toujours ivre. Tout est là: c'est l'unique question. Pour ne pas sentir l'horrible fardeau du Temps qui brise vos épaules et vous penche vers la terre, il faut vous enivrer sans trêve.

   Mais de quoi? De vin, de poésie ou de vertu, à votre guise. Mais enivrez-vous.

   Et si quelquefois, sur les marches d'un palais, sur l'herbe verte d'un fossé, dans la solitude morne de votre chambre, vous vous réveillez, l'ivresse déjà diminuée ou disparue, demandez au vent, à la vague, à l'étoile, à l'horloge, à tout ce qui fuit, à tout ce qui gémit, à tout ce qui roule, à tout ce qui chante, à tout ce qui parle, demandez quelle heure il est; et le vent, la vague, l'étoile, l'oiseau, l'horloge, vous répondront: "Il est l'heure de s'enivrer! Pour n'être pas les esclaves martyrisés du Temps, enivrez-vous; enivrez-vous sans cesse! De vin, de poésie ou de vertu, à votre guise."

[XXXIII
Get Drunk

   One must be drunk at all times. Everything's there: it's the only question. So as not to feel the horrible burden of Time that's crushing your shoulders and bending you down to the earth, you must be unremittingly drunk.

   But on what? On wine, on poetry, or on virtue, as you wish. But get drunk.

   And if sometime, on the steps of a palace, on the green grass of a ditch, in the dismal solitude of your room, you awaken, your drunkenness going or gone, ask the wind, the wave, the star, the bird, the clock, all that flees, all that moans, all that rolls, all that sings, all that speaks, ask what time it is; and the wind, the wave, the star, the bird, the clock, will answer: "It's time to get drunk! So as not to be the martyred slaves of Time, get drunk; get ceaselessly drunk. On wine, on poetry, or on virtue, as you wish."]

We may note, first of all, that in both pieces praise takes a backseat to instruction: the reader is *commanded*—To do what? Not "Know thyself," or "Seize the day," or "Question authority," but "Get drunk," "Enivrez-vous." This compacting of the grammatical form of instruction, the imperative, with a thematics of intoxication turns inside out the commonplace picture of poetry as combining a pleasing form with an instructive content.

Beyond the common substance of this open charge, there are distinct similarities in the way both pieces play out its rule. First of all, both begin—let us set aside Baudelaire's heading for the moment—with a declarative maxim ("Man, being reasonable, must get drunk"; "Il faut être toujours ivre"), which only after some rhetorical to and fro issues in the force of an actual command: "But to return, get very drunk"; "Mais enivrez-vous."

Second, in both the imperative moment leads precipitously to the picturing of a scene not of inebriation, but of its aftermath or interruption: "When you wake with headache . . . "; "Et si quelquefois . . . vous vous reveillez, l'ivresse déjà diminuée ou disparue . . . " At this point the interval or scene of intoxication itself is marked by its elision from the sequence of representations.

Finally, the prospect of waking, which hangs like a question or doubt over the initial command, prompts in both cases a supplemental prescription, this time not a single compressed rule, but a linked series of instructions that cross over from the writer's framing injunction to the reader into the projected aftermath and end up repeating and transposing, as into another key, the initial command.

If the performative force of both pieces—what happens through their writing—is bound up with, first, the issuing of a trangressive injunction and second, the pattern of insistence and displacement whose outlines we have just traced, this is not to say that in delivering their message both pack the same punch. In what follows, I look more closely at each in turn to ask what their repetitions show us emerging in Romanticism's wake. I begin by calling attention to the ways Byron's freewheeling assimilation and parody of a range of rhetorical models is strung out, so to speak, by a compulsive orality that pursues its fitful labors at a subgeneric—and a fortiori subheroic—

level of cultural conflict, transmission, and transformation. And then I suggest specific ways Baudelaire's writing radicalizes the desublimating materialization of language already conspicuous in Byron's poetry or, in de Man's formulation, "bring[s] out the prosaic element that shaped the poems in the first place" (*Aesthetic Ideology*, 153).[4]

Starting then with the first line of Byron's minisermon: "Man, being reasonable, must get drunk," one can dignify this dictum with a sober paraphrase, but doing so too quickly risks throwing out the baby with the bathos. For its transgressive humor has less to do with its libertine challenge to received moral wisdom than with the way the sentence juxtaposes almost without mediation two incongruous levels of diction: the sententiousness of "Man, being reasonable, must . . ." and the common slang "get drunk."[5] On the one hand, that final blurt ambushes the lumbering sentence and robs it of its gravitas. On the other hand, and here the plot thickens, it also condenses within itself the sentence it disrupts. This is partly a matter of grammar, since the two words "get drunk" constitute in themselves, as I have noted, an imperative sentence in which a binding command to ingest a substance is intertwined with an unbinding invitation to self-forgetting transport, and it is partly a matter of rhythm and sound, since "drunk" echoes "must" and the dactyls, diphthongs, and polysyllables of "Man, being reasonable" harden into the monosyllabic thumping—one syllable per word and one beat per syllable—of "must get drunk."

Thus, although I began by suggesting that the line's transgressive force has less to do with what it says than with the way it abruptly downshifts from lofty to low, I now want to double back on that suggestion. For the coordinated effects of register, rhythm, sound, and grammar that we have been looking at, effects that trip up the balance of a certain cadence of moral generalization and in so doing pitch it forward, devolve into the idiom of oral excess not as one "low" mode among others, but as a totalizing code with a privilege and pull of its own.[6] Some stanzas earlier in canto 2, in a sequence that is in some respects a grotesque send-up of "The Ancient Mariner," the starving crew of a becalmed ship draws lots to determine who among them is going to be sacrificed and cannibalized so the others can survive. Juan's "pastor and master" (2.624), Pedrillo, is the hapless victim, and tracing the fate of the tutor's corpse through the varying stages of its depredation provides Byron with a fair amount of narrative material, beginning with an account of getting drunk by the surgeon who bleeds him to death:

> The surgeon, as there was no other fee
>   Had his first choice of morsels for his pains;

But being thirstiest at the moment, he
　Preferr'd a draught from the fast-flowing veins.　(2.609–12)

I offer this sequence as evidence that a lively phantasmagorics of incorporative violence lurks in the vicinity of the dictum we have been pondering. Indeed, read against the background of Pedrillo's fate, one might even hear that dictum as articulating a civilizing prohibition and substitution: man affirms his "reasonable" nature in suppressing his cannibalistic impulses and accepting the substitution of wine for human blood. Thus, in the episode just cited Juan's fastidiousness, which sets him apart from the crew, is marked by his refusal to partake of his tutor's remains, a refusal resulting in part from lingering disgust at having already eaten his pet spaniel. The crew members, for their part, end up going mad.[7] The morality of *Don Juan*, it seems, is in many ways a matter of dietary code.

Which is in a sense my point. But rather than simply placing Byron's stanzas in the context of some master myth about the savage origins of civil society, à la *Totem and Taboo,* let me be more specific about some of the factors, cultural, psychological, and formal, that I see conditioning their oral compulsions. In the verses immediately preceding the two stanzas I have excerpted, Byron celebrates wine of old vintage and belittles those who preach:

Few things surpass old wine; and they may preach
　Who please,—the more because they preach in vain,—
Let us have wine and women, mirth and laughter,
Sermons and soda-water the day after.　(2.1421–24)

Having explicitly mocked the preachers as verbally impotent, powerless to place under their sway the desires of either men or women, Byron then offers a bravura display of his own *virtu,* what Jerome Christensen has written about so well under the title *Lord Byron's Strength,* by launching into a mock sermon, blithely appropriating, for spectacularly unauthorized purposes, bits and pieces of the code of pious predication—its tone, its formulas, and some of its fund of scriptural allusion. (I am thinking here in particular of the biblical figure of the tree of life [cf. "life's strange tree"][8] and the related commandment to "be fruitful and multiply.") On the one hand, I follow Christensen's lead in seeing this performance as asserting an older symbolic economy of expenditure and extravagant consumption associated with aristocratic privilege ("few things surpass old wine") over against a commercialist economy of production, trade, and accumulation, though doing so in what is in some ways a postrevolutionary context and with the hope of sharing that privilege with a vaster community through their participation in his poetry and the tragicomic drama of his life.[9]

Again, in terms of English cultural history and intertwined with the shifting class structures, one can see Byron appealing to an older religious dispensation, associated with Catholicism and organized around a sacramental communion, over against a newer Protestant order in which sermon and hymn displace the sacrament as a focus of ritual gathering.

Conflicting identifications permit Byron to deploy aristocratic privilege and sensitivity to distinctions of rank in the name of an ostensibly radical attack on Southey and the Lake Poets for having "turn'd out a Tory at Last" (3–4) and offering in their writings "'A dainty dish to set before the King,' / Or Regent, who admires such kind of food" (11–12), as he quips in the dedication to *Don Juan*. But these identifications would be both politically and poetically without significance were they not underwritten by a psychological and linguistic adherence to a pre-Oedipal dynamic of self-definition, unstable in itself, that in turn destabilized his relation to the transmission of patriarchal authority.[10]

We have already seen expressions of this vexed pattern of conflict—an Oedipal pattern of contestation and identification between subjects defined by their shared difference from the object they contest devolving into a pre-Oedipal structure of ambivalent identification with the object—in the clash of registers we noted earlier and in the way the closing words "get drunk" condense within themselves the volatility of that clash. The lines that follow and that are supposed to prove the truth of the opening maxim process the conflict, with the marks of ambivalence particularly strong around those words that have to do with vessels and fluids.

Thus the one-sentence verse immediately following, "The best of life is but intoxication," is morose ("Vanity of vanities, saith the Preacher, vanity of vanities; all is vanity") rather than cheering, with the word "intoxication" being used pejoratively to diminish and negate any locus of appeal, its own included. And in the two-line sentence that follows that, "Glory, the grape, love, gold, in these are sunk / The hopes of every man and every nation," the crisp enumeration of worldly goods is followed by a good deal of lexical and syntactical ambiguity focused on "sunk," the rhyme word to "drunk." Does "sunk" mean "lost in a fluid medium," like someone drowned or a ship at sea, or the symmetrical swallowing up of the drinker by the fluid substance he imbibes? Or does it connote investment in an object of speculation that may yield a return, as when we speak of the sinking of capital into a venture, or again, the anchoring of roots in some ground or source of nutriment, a fertilizing act of sexual impregnation, or "the expense of spirit in a waste of shame"? The semantic overdeterminations that make the word "sunk" in this context so heavy and laden as a word are connected with an ambiguity in the preposition "in." Do the four nouns name containers, bounded vessels "in" which boundless hopes are placed, whether for safekeeping, for transfer, or for loss, or are the hopes themselves things that are lost in the voids of "glory" and so on? Are the names themselves vessels of meaning, or does each open onto a boundlessness that may be both threatening and wondrous?

In evoking the semantic and psychic turmoil that swirls around the word "sunk" in these two lines, I do not mean that Byron's meaning does not "tilt," if you will, in a particular direction. The affirmative, if ironic, tendency of the statement is clear as we see it moving from the ecclesiastical mournfulness of the preceding line to the celebratory exclamation of those that follow: "Without their sap, how branchless were the trunk / Of life's strange tree, so fruitful on occasion!" This movement toward affirmation is clearly connected, though, to the articulation of the "drinking" motif with figurations of phallic potency and multiplication, as these ward off the threat of a "branchless trunk." In particular the word "sap," with its antithetical connotations of draining and of infusing with regenerative force, takes over from "sunk" as a switch word and provides the needed verbal crossover from wasteful drinking to seminal fluid. Though even here the initial incorporative motif hangs around, as it were, in the fruit that may or may not be the branches themselves.

My point is that Byron's verse gravitates to a figure of virile proliferation in order to resolve the ambivalences carried by the incorporative language and also that this resolution is notably momentary. For the words "But to return" that preface the actual imperative ("—Get very drunk . . .") and that follow on the mounting declamations, while bringing us back to the opening maxim, though now rather emptied of its figurative juices, are also an acknowledgment that the speaker has been carried away by the transporting flow of his own words, that is, that there has been a conspicuous and self-induced lapse of rhetorical control. The moment of command and direct address thus occurs within the movement of the verse as a "coming to" and a prefiguration of the moment when the reader, having followed the poet's instructions, "wakes with headache" in an indoor setting that peremptorily displaces the expansive natural imagery of the previous stanza.

The connection between the two moments is clear from the way Byron, along with his hangover, transfers to his projected reader (clearly styled as a man of the ruling class, though Byron's actual readership was of course nei-

ther solely male nor predominantly of the same class as he was) the prerogative of command: "Ring for your valet—bid him quickly bring / Some hock
and soda-water, then you'll know / A pleasure worthy Xerxes the great king."
The linked chain of commands—the poet commanding his reader to command his servant's presence so that he may then command the servant to
bring him a dialectically balanced mixture of hock and soda water—places
in view a definite and graduated symbolic hierarchy: the poet writes out a
prescription for a lordly reader who, from a position that is one of both repose and incapacitation, is to issue oral instructions to his servant, who in
turn is to discharge his instructions not by speaking but, in a physical action
analogous to his own summoning, by going and bringing from outside the
room something inanimate and ingestible. Obviously Byron is inviting the
reader to participate, by identification if not in fact, in some of the dubious
privileges of his lordship. But in taking leave of this passage I want to emphasize the ambiguity of Byron's position as a *writer* in relation to this briefly
conjured master-servant scene and note just how quickly that scene is sub-
sumed in a hyperbolic exaltation of the power of the incorporated object.

BY WAY of transition to Baudelaire, I offer a little tale, not from the crypt,
but from the main reading room of the New York Public Library. Here are
some things I discovered in the library and some that I didn't:

"Enivrez-vous" was first published on 7 February 1864 along with three
others of Baudelaire's prose poems, followed by two more the following
week, in a literary journal called *Le Figaro*. The journal initially told its readers that the series was to be continued in subsequent issues, but the director,
Villemessant, informed the poet, as Baudelaire reported it in a letter to his
mother (*Correspondance*, 2:350 and editorial note 844), that his prose poems
"ennuyaient tout le monde" [bored everyone] and discontinued their publication in his pages. A more recent and more pointed dropping out occurs
in Margery Evans's 1993 study of the prose poems, *Baudelaire and Intertextuality*, which indexes the prose poems numerically rather than alphabeti-
cally, using the roman numerals that have accompanied Baudelaire's titles
from the time of the collection's initial, and posthumous, publication. In
Fusées Baudelaire writes: "*Tout* est nombre. Le nombre est dans *tout*. Le nombre est dans l'individu. L'ivresse est une nombre" [*All* is number. Number is
in *all*. Number is in the individual. Intoxication is a number] (*Oeuvres complètes*, 1:649). The number "XXXIII," as it happens, if we may judge by the
place occupied by "Enivrez-vous" in the final collection, and whose soterio-

logical significance seems all the more likely if we consider that Baudelaire played with the idea of titling "Le Serpent tout entier" (*Oeuvres complètes*, 1:275), the tortuous fantasy of his collection, "Les 66" (*Oeuvres complètes*, 1:365).

Be that as it may, when I consulted the index of Evans's work to see what she might have to say about "Enivrez-vous" and possibly the connection with Byron, there seemed to be no "XXXIII, Enivrez-vous" for my finger to alight on. I thus went one by one in order through all the numbers, and they were all there, I through L, all but XXXIII, which had evidently been "oublié sur la carte." On the other hand, another recent commentator whose work I consulted, Edward Kaplan, not only offers a discussion of the prose poem but refers to it as "this celebrated escapist manifesto" (*Baudelaire's Prose Poems*, 118). This judgment seems to be supported by the fact, recently reported to me by Jeff Cassvan, that Dustin Hoffman recited the poem in translation as part of a tribute to Jack Nicholson broadcast on cable. Paul Celan compared poetry to a message in a bottle, meaning, in my understanding, to say something of its interiority, its vulnerability, and as Derrida has stressed, the utter contingency and singularity of the poem's encounter with its reader. In this case it seems that the bottle, at any rate, has found its way to shore.

I recall the details of my slightly Borgesian experience with Evans's index not, I hope, as an exercise in critical one-upsmanship, but to show how implacable and unnegotiable these particular words may be, particularly when compared with the boffo theatricality of Byron's satire. The time and place out of which they speak is both nearer to us and more mythic, more akin perhaps to that of the satyr Silenus, foster father of Dionysus, in a story retold by Nietzsche early in *The Birth of Tragedy*. Captured after long hunting by King Midas and asked, "What is the best thing for mortals?" Silenus first curses the one who has bound and questioned him. And then he answers with vengeful fury, "What is best of all is utterly beyond your reach: not to be born, not to be, to be nothing. But the second best for you is—to die soon."

In this spirit, and here we can begin to measure some of the differences between Baudelaire's prose and Byron's poetic treatment of his theme, the first paragraph of "Enivrez-vous" eschews any appeal in the name of reason or simulation of the rhythms of proof. One confronts instead a series of bluntly apodictic statements that allow neither place ("Tout est là: c'est l'unique question") nor time ("Il faut être toujours ivre"; "il faut vous enivrer sans trêve") for alternatives or gradations. Their unrelenting insistence is a mirror image of the "dictatorship of time" that Baudelaire evokes at the end of "La Chambre double": "Oui! le Temps règne; il a repris sa brutale dictature. Et il me pousse, comme si j'étais un boeuf, avec son double aiguillon.—'Et hue donc, bourrique! Sue donc, esclave! Vis donc, damné!'" [Yes! Time reigns; it has reinstated its brutal dictatorship. And it drives me, as though I were an ox, with its double goad.—"So gee-up now, ass! So sweat, slave! So live, damned one!"].[11] Nor does Baudelaire align the powers of figural language with the potent appeal of the drug.[12] Rather, figuration is used in the first instance to register the obliterative pressure of the destructive and all but inescapable weight of time: "Pour ne pas sentir l'horrible fardeau du Temps qui brise vos épaules et vous penche vers la terre, il faut vous enivrer sans trêve."

The image itself is arrestingly clear—we can all picture what it means to bend under the weight of a crushing burden—and we understand too, if more implicitly, the symbolic coordinates in which the human figure is being situated, turned away from the open heavens and toward the earth into which it is being broken down, between the past that is behind it and weighs it down and a mortal future toward which we move. One may think of the leech gatherer of "Resolution and Independence," whose appearance concretizes for the poet his own anxieties about the fate awaiting him:

> His body . . . bent double, feet and head
> Coming together in life's pilgrimage;
> As if some dire constraint of pain, or rage
> Of sickness felt by him in times long past,
> A more than human weight upon his frame had cast.   (66–70)

Yet if the totalizing claim of the image as an emblem of the human condition in all its generality is understandable in these terms, in the picturing of not just the past but time itself as a massive, inert burden there is a residual strangeness that resists this reading, a strangeness that may be most quickly brought out if we contrast Baudelaire's objectification with the more familiar and intuitively more comprehensible figure of time as something flowing—perhaps in raging destruction, but flowing nonetheless.

This reification is of a piece with the foregrounding of the word "Temps" itself by its capitalization, an orthographic stress that verges on allegorical personification.[13] Antithetical counterpart to the totalizing figure of the drug, as it gathers an unnumbered multiplicity of desires and objects of desire under one (be-)heading ("Tout est là"), the reifying picture of time as massive and oppressive object similarly marks the poetic impulse to abolish the difference between word and object, but with this difference: the word functions not as an object of attraction, but as a phobic object that both reflects and resists the violence of the desire for representational immediacy and control. The nature of this representational violence and the specificity of its relation to the question of time should not be understood, except figurally, in terms of the desire to make an absent or distant object present. It should be seen, more fundamentally, in terms of the constitution of a phantasmatic object that can come into being only through a denial of the merely verbal—and as such indifferent to the rules of spatiotemporal ordering—possibilities of connection that it nonetheless exploits. The figure of time as inert burden is produced by the resistance of the word itself to the mastery of figural understanding.

To the extent that the absoluteness of this figure and the declarations in which it is embedded seek to impose their authority while challenging comprehension, they generate a question. And again in some contrast with the excerpt from *Don Juan,* the matter of questioning figures as repeatedly in "Enivrez-vous" as that of commanding. We encounter it first in the second sentence of the opening paragraph: "Tout est là: c'est l'unique question." We can of course glide over this phrase as one more way of saying "That's the key," but since everything up to this point has been a statement rather than a question, one may well ask exactly what Baudelaire is referring to as "the sole question," so that the statement gives rise to further questions while seeming to foreclose them. Moreover, following fast on the "sole question" named in the opening, a second question is not only referred to but voiced in the opening words of the second paragraph: "Mais de quoi?" I say voiced rather than posed, since it is clear that the question is staged as an anticipatory mirroring of a question represented as originating not with the writer but with the reader, and that this mirroring fends off the question as much as it entertains a dialogue. The seemingly urbane answer that follows, "De vin, de poésie ou de vertu, à votre guise," thus confounds the wish to differentiate literal from metaphoric intoxication, poetry from wine (whereas poetry is notably absent from Byron's list of intoxicants ["Glory, the grape, love, gold"], indicating not the absence of a reflexive linguistic turn but the need to keep it implicit). But it also treats "virtue," the renunciation of all intoxication, as yet one more means of intoxication, leaving it uncertain if there is any position of questioning or resistance that Baudelaire's text has not sought to predesignate as a confirmation of its rule. The imperative moment that follows this baffling play of question and response ("Mais enivrez-vous") thus simply displaces the opening question ("Mais de quoi?"), but in so doing it renders itself all the more enigmatic. Well might Nietzsche ask, "Wer ist Dionysus?"

As I noted earlier, the explicit prescription, once it does occur, leads directly, as in Byron, to the scripting of a scene of awakening: "Et si quelquefois, sur l'herbe verte d'une fossé, sur les marches d'un palais, dans la solitude morne de votre chambre, vous vous reveillez, l'ivresse déjà diminuée ou disparue." One could dwell at length on the symbolic resonances coded by each of these three scenes of forlornness and the forms of interrelation suggested by the rhythm of their succession, beginning with "l'herbe verte d'une fossé," with its simultaneous suggestions of rebirth and abandonment, and moving via the interrupted architectonic of "les marches d'un palais" to the monotonous, tomblike confinement of "la solitude morne de votre chambre." Here we need only observe that the choice and multiplication of scenes leaves the social position of both writer and reader far less determinate than does the comparable moment in *Don Juan*. Correlated with this dislocation of social identity are two further differences. There is no valet, and since there is no valet, there is no one handy to order about. And if in Byron character and setting are specified, so is the moment: "When you wake with headache," the pain of headache punctually marking the end and other of intoxication. In "Enivrez-vous," a punctual sense of temporal location is especially what is wanting. The paragraph opens not with "and when" but rather with "and if at some time," "et si quelquefois," and the modifying phrase that follows ("vous vous reveillez"—"l'ivresse déjà diminuée ou disparue") evokes the possibility of a temporal blurring where up till now everything has been a matter of sharp contrast. Baudelaire's supplemental instruction, "demandez . . . quelle heure il est," thus occurs within an interval of waking disorientation (not unlike that of the opening paragraphs of *A la recherche du temps perdu*) before the ordering of time has resumed.

The instruction to ask (which, to repeat, occurs in Baudelaire whereas in Byron there is an instruction to summon and command) is formulated in a way that further opens up the interval in which it is posed, since we are told at length what we should address our question to before we are told, with a reiteration of "demandez" that recalls us to the governing imperative, what we are to ask—namely, what time it is.

What we are told to question in this interval are nonhuman entities: inanimate, animate, earthly, heavenly, natural, man-made, but in any case not human. As with the series of three scenes referred to earlier, the series of five things and then of five verbs invites considerable interpretative speculation. This speculation includes whether and how particular verbs can be correlated with particular nouns and whether the sequence forms some kind of symbolic progression to be deciphered—perhaps even a brief history of time, to borrow Stephen Hawking's title—or functions simply as a monotonous, perhaps hypnotic, enumeration, a verbal equivalent of the mesmerizer's swaying, ticking watch. Again I will limit myself to the observation that we can associate the bird, which sings ("tout ce qui chante") and can suspend itself in flight, with lyric poetry and the clock, which speaks ("tout ce qui parle"), albeit mechanically, in telling the time (the etymology of *horloge* being "speaking the hour"), with the domain of prose. Thus the hybrid mode of Baudelaire's prose poem would be figured, minimally, in the compounding of bird and clock. Pursuing this thought, one might think of the verbal artifact Baudelaire has patiently fashioned out of, and to lend voice to, the madness of impatience as a kind of cuckoo clock.

As I noted earlier, the identification of poet and reader in *Don Juan* is at least momentarily styled as a shared participation in the privilege of command, an identification that entails as its corollary the figure of a mute obedient servant and, subordinate to the labor of that servant, the substance he transports for our consumption and by which we are then overpowered. In its mediating displacements, this structure is hierarchical and analogical in a way that perpetuates the rhetorical movement of the first stanza's "proof" and that alternately is propped up by and drives the nonsemantic, but fundamentally oral, flow of rhyming that keeps *Don Juan* going and seeks to carry the reader along with it.

Returning to "Enivrez-vous," we may observe first that Baudelaire has written his poem in prose, that is, has foregone marked adherence to the rhythms of verse. Second, we see that the relationship between writer and addressee is asymmetrical: the writer commands the projected reader not to command, but to ask, and that query is to be directed not along a chain of subordination to someone who mediates the reader's relation to things but directly and fantastically to things themselves. Third, we note that the projected interval into which the reader's question is prescribed is one in which the waking consciousness has not yet located itself in time. Generalizing, we may say that the movement of Baudelaire's language is away from a triangulated structure of intersubjective identification and toward a more enigmatic, nonintersubjective exchange with things, at once hallucinatory and utterly prosaic. For we all, everyday, consult the clock to tell us what time it is, and there is hardly a question more everyday in its function and more formulaic in its wording than the one we are instructed to ask: "Quelle heure il est?"

Finally, whereas the stanzas we excerpted from *Don Juan* culminate in the hyperbolic exaltation of an actual drink, "Enivrez-vous" moves beyond hyperbole to the surreal divination of a universe of talking things, all of which renew the poem's imperative, though with certain alterations. For one thing, there is a change in the way the pronoun *vous* functions. Up till this moment, it is grammatically ambiguous whether Baudelaire has been using *vous* as a plural pronoun of address or as the polite form of the singular: *vous* rather than *tu*. But with the phrase "Pour n'être pas les esclaves martyrisés du Temps, enivrez-vous," the address becomes unmistakably plural, everything is speaking to everyone in a mad proclamation that is both mute and totally open. The concentrated authority of the commanding voice that inaugurates the poem thus explodes in an ecstatic *feu d'artifice* that is quite amazing. Yet the verbal means by which this unbinding happens are evidently mechanical, consisting mainly in the use of prosopopeia—the attribution of voice to nonspeaking entities—and remind us of the detachment that was so much a part of Baudelaire's relation to words and to his readership. That detachment is available to a wide range of affective coloration—as the violence of mastery, as the vengeful indifference of forced and alienated labor, or its hopeless despair, as obsessional manipulation, or as the trancelike loosening of thought and feeling that so often informs the performance of prosaic tasks—but in any case it is an engagement with the object of labor in its materiality before it is intersubjective.

*

On a pensé, de nos jours, que les *horloges* étaient faites surtout pour marquer l'heure, et au lieu de s'amuser à multiplier tous ses joujoux, propres seulement à amuser les enfants et à troubler le méchanisme, on s'est attaché à perfectionner la forme, le fini du travail, et l'on a pu atteindre ainsi une perfection que nos ancêtres n'avaient pas même rêvée.

[In our day, the thinking is that clocks were made above all to mark the hour, and instead of idly multiplying all these toys, the focus has been on perfecting the form and finish of the work, and we have thus attained to a perfection our ancestors had not even dreamed of.] (From the entry "L'Horloge" in the *Grand Dictionnaire universel du XIXe siècle*)

I conclude with a comment on the historical specificity of Baudelaire's piece. In addition to the literary resonance with Byron we started out from, there is strong evidence that "Enivrez-vous" is a distant (and mocking) echo of the political slogan "Enrichissez-vous"[14] (a truncation of a longer formula, "Enrichessez-vous par le travail et l'épargne" [Get rich through work and saving]), which figured prominently in the electoral debates in the 1840s over extending suffrage to the millions of disfranchised French citizens who did not pay the two hundred francs in property taxes that was a condition of suffrage under the constitutional monarchy of Louis-Philippe. In consequence the actual electoral base was closer to 240,000, a central issue in precipitating the revolution of 1848 (Broglie, *Guizot,* 333–44). The author of this formula, François Guizot (whose name perhaps makes a furtive appearance in Baudelaire's piece in the twice-repeated sequence " . . . de vertu, à votre guise") was not only minister of the interior and of foreign affairs under Louis-Philippe but a prolific historian ("[Michelet] s'est plaint de sa réputation d'être en histoire la Poésie, alors que Guizot personnifiait la Prose" [Michelet complained of his reputation as the Poetry of history, while Guizot personified the Prose]) [Broglie, *Guizot,* 424]). He also played a key role in creating France's public education system, at the same time that he staunchly defended restricting suffrage to those who had accumulated a certain stake in the existing economy (see Rosanvallon, "Guizot et la question du suffrage"). He is mentioned by Marx as one of the first theoreticians of history as class conflict (quoted by Hoeges, *François Guizot,* 138) and targeted by name in the opening salvo of *The Communist Manifesto.*

More speculatively, I would venture an association between Baudelaire's piece and the textual device of another writer, the educational and economic theorist, and political figure of the period, Marc-Antoine Jullien. Among his other writings, Jullien was the author of a voluminous work, first published in 1808, titled *Essai sur l'emploi du temps,* which sketches a rudimentary theory of surplus value based on the distinction between the time necessary to minister to one's basic needs (likened to a "fund destined for immediate consumption") and the time that then remains (which, in its proper use, functions like "capital employed to produce an income"). A kind of grid that Jullien had appended to his volume for readers' practical application of his theories on the use of time acquired a publication life of it own and apparently enjoyed something of a vogue lasting into the 1830s under the name "biomètre" or "montre morale" [moral timepiece]. Divided into days along one axis and then into various categories ("physical," "moral," "intellectual," and "social") and subcategories along the other, with space left in the right margin for the user's self-monitoring comments, its purported function was to guide one in the productive and exhaustive organization of one's time and, presumably, to provide a portable text-object one could consult to determine what one should be doing at any particular time: hence the name "montre morale" (Palmer, *From Jacobin to Liberal*, 155–58, 206, 237).

I have no evidence that Baudelaire ever either saw or heard of Jullien's contrivance. Yet there is a striking affinity between his "montre moral" and Baudelaire's cuckoo clock of a prose poem that, whenever we consult it about the time, will tell us "C'est l'heure de s'enivrer!" It is not hard to see that there is a kind of madness in the methodical binding of time as capital for investment that Jullien's device seeks to make available in a commodified text. It is harder, perhaps, to see that there is poetry bound up in the madness of his moral timepiece. "Enivrez-vous" winds it to its breaking point.

Eight

"Le Bonheur Vomitif"

Incorporation and Figuration in
Baudelaire's "Poème du Hachisch"

Often admired from afar, *Les Paradis artificiels* has always been among the more curious of Baudelaire's "curiosités esthétiques." Writing to Baudelaire shortly after its publication, for example, Flaubert hailed the book as "le commencement d'une *science* . . . une oeuvre d'observation et d'induction" ["the beginning of a *science* . . . a work of observation and induction"]. But precisely because he saw it as advancing the standard of science into uncharted territory, he was disconcerted to note in its prose the tokens of another allegiance:

> Vous avez (et à plusieurs reprises) insisté trop (?) sur *l'Esprit du Mal.* On sent comme un levain de catholicisme çà et là. J'aurais mieux aimé que vous ne *blâmiez pas* le haschisch, l'opium, l'excès. Savez-vous ce qui en sortira plus tard?

> [You have (and on several occasions) laid too much stress (?) on *the Spirit of Evil.* One picks up a whiff of Catholicism here and there. I would have preferred it had you *not condemned* hashish, opium, excess. Do you know what will emerge from them later?] (Baudelaire, *Correspondance,* 1:1379n)

Although Flaubert takes Baudelaire to task for condemning drugs in religious terms, the terms of his own criticism nonetheless mirror those of Baudelaire's denunciation: for in Flaubert's characterization, Baudelaire's recurrent references to "L'Esprit du Mal" betray the operation within an otherwise sober work of investigation of a heterogeneous agent of fermentation and expansion, "un levain"—a whiff, a germ, a leavening—"de catholicisme." Flaubert's polite restraint notwithstanding, the operative symbolic economy is clear: Catholicism exchanges places with drugs as the object of rhetorical exorcism, in full keeping with Marx's balder polemical identification of religion as the opiate of the people. Such is the irrepressible insistence of the *pharmakos,* and it is with the gathered force of that insistence that Baudelaire was to respond to Flaubert's comments:

> J'ai été frappé de votre observation, et étant descendu tres sincèrement dans le souvenir de mes rêveries, je me suis aperçu que de tout temps j'ai été obsédé par l'impossibilité de me rendre compte de certaines actions ou pensées soudaines de l'homme sans l'hypothèse de l'intervention d'une force méchante extérieure à lui.—Voilà un gros aveu dont tout le 19e siècle conjuré ne me fera pas rougir.
>
> [I was struck by your observation, and having descended very sincerely into the memory of my reveries, I realized that I have always been haunted by the impossibility of accounting for certain of man's sudden actions or thoughts without the hypothesis of the intervention of an external evil force.—Here is a blunt admission for which not the whole assembled nineteenth century can make me blush.] (*Correspondance,* 1:1379n)

One may of course see this reply and the defiant avowal it concludes with as yet one more reactionary adherence on Baudelaire's part to a dated set of beliefs. But his redoubled espousal of precisely the form of language Flaubert asks him to abjure is just as clearly an expression of critical resistance to his century's confident belief in the imperial progress of knowledge and industry.[1] As Nietzsche was to emphasize, the underlying logic of this belief was that of an askesis, a progressive purification through negation, and Baudelaire's response situates his language, his thought, and his very person in the position of the expelled element on whose continuing negation that askesis depends. The exchange of letters between Flaubert and Baudelaire is, then, only superficially a debate between two conflicting judgments. On a more fundamental level, Baudelaire's insistence on identifying drugs with the satanic issues from a position radically "exterior" to the field of discourse within which such a debate might take place.[2]

The demonization of drugs that Flaubert flagged is of a piece with Baudelaire's even more conspicuous beatification of poetic labor, a beatification that Flaubert passes over but that explicitly constitutes the moral of "Le Poème du hachisch" (the fifth and final section of which is titled "Morale") and, in the view of some readers, its true raison d'être. Thus Michel Butor has argued for a reading of the work as Baudelaire's fundamental statement on the "absolute drug of poetry" ("cette drogue absolue qu'est la poésie" ["Les Paradis artificiels," 10]):

> Les Paradis artificiels, livre que Baudelaire a écrit sur deux drogues: le haschisch et l'opium, joue par conséquent, dans l'ensemble de son oeuvre, un rôle très précis. Il est son ouvrage fondamental sur la nature de la poésie, et les deux produits en question y jouent le rôle de deux grandes images à quoi il va pouvoir la comparer puis l'opposer.

> [Les Paradis artificiels, a book Baudelaire wrote on two drugs, hashish and opium, as a result plays a very precise role in the totality of his oeuvre. It is his fundamental work on the nature of poetry, and the two products in question play the role of two great images to which he will be able to compare and then oppose it.] (11)

In this passage, as in Butor's reading of the book as a whole, the difference between poetry and drugs is essentially a difference of means rather than of ends: drugs seek by "a single stroke" to achieve the ecstatic transcendence the poet attains through arduous spiritual labor. And it is precisely to the extent that the writing of poetry is imagined as the self-affecting use of language to achieve a higher state of consciousness that the intoxicating drug offers itself as a figure to which poetry may, as Butor says, be compared and then opposed.

The dichotomy Butor evokes is most clearly in evidence in the exquisite allegorical tableau with which Baudelaire closes "Le Poème du hachisch" (Oeuvres complètes, 1:441), a tableau in which the somber Apollonian calm of the poet (also variously identified as "a Brahman" and "a Christian philosopher")[3] who has ascended by means of "long fasts and assiduous prayers" ("longs jeûnes et . . . prières assidues") "the arduous Olympus of spirituality" ("l'Olympe ardu de la spiritualité") is contrasted with the twisted grimaces and spasmodic cries of the drugged multitude thronging its base, the "band of helots" ("la bande des ilotes") who "seek from black magic the means to raise themselves to supernatural existence by a single stroke" ("demandent à la noire magie les moyens de s'élever, d'un seul coup, à l'existence surnaturelle").

Yet in an essay published shortly before Butor's, and to which the latter was perhaps responding, Maurice Saillet had argued that, its moral cover notwithstanding, *Les Paradis artificiels* was covert testimony to Baudelaire's poetic debt to drugs ("Baudelaire et l'épreuve des excitants," 99, 102–3). The poet's Pléiade editors arrive at a related, if somewhat perplexed, conclusion: "L'excitant est un adjuvant. C'est ce que Baudelaire laisse entendre à son lecteur. Sinon, à quoi bon écrire un livre de trois cents pages?" [Stimulants are supplements. This is what Baudelaire leads his reader to understand. Otherwise why write a three-hundred-page book?] (*Oeuvres complètes,* 1:1365n). And many another commentator has remarked, more or less ruefully, on the tension between the book's declared ethical mission and its seductive description of intoxicated states.[4]

More recently, and working on a more textual level of analysis, Claire Lyu has observed in an insightful essay on Baudelaire's "high poetics" how "the text [of 'Le Poème du hachisch'] constantly oscillates between the desire and the attempt to keep poetry and hashish separate, on the one hand, and the failure in marking and maintaining the difference between these two, on the other" ("'High Poetics,'" 700). Lyu focuses primarily on the precariousness of the structural division between "the poet's sober voice" (699) and "the intoxicated voices" (701) who report their experiences with hashish in the third section of the work, "Le Théâtre de Séraphin," a division all the more precarious if, following Saillet, one reads the latter voices as masking what are at bottom autobiographical accounts.[5] But perhaps the most striking instance of the collapse of this division occurs toward the end of the fourth section, "L'Homme-dieu," in which Baudelaire constructs a hypothetical subject best suited to tracing the evolution of the drug's moral effects, and whom he designates as "la forme banale de l'originalité" [the banal form of originality] (*Oeuvres complètes,* 1:429–30), a coinage that might equally suit his prose poetry. Having traced this evolution to its penultimate phase of grandiosity, Baudelaire pauses to ask:

Cela ne vous fait-il pas souvenir de Jean-Jacques, qui, lui aussi, après s'être confessé à l'univers, non sans une certaine volupté, a osé pousser le même cri de triomphe (ou du moins la différence est bien petite) avec la même sincérité et la même conviction? L'enthousiasme avec lequel il admirait la vertu, l'attendrissement nerveux qui remplissait ses yeux de larmes, à la vue d'une belle action ou à la pensée de toutes les belles actions qu'il aurait voulu accomplir, suffisaient pour lui donner une idée superlative de sa valeur moral. Jean-Jacques s'était enivré sans hachisch.

[Doesn't this remind you of Jean-Jacques, who also, after having made his confession to the universe, not without a certain thrill of pleasure, dared to let out the same triumphal cry (or at least the difference is quite small) with the same sincerity and the same conviction? The enthusiasm with which he admired virtue, the nervous tenderness that filled his eyes with tears at the sight of a beautiful action or at the thought of all the beautiful actions he would have liked to perform, were sufficient to give him a superlative idea of his own moral value. Jean-Jacques intoxicated himself without hashish.] (1:436)

This is the anxiety of being-under-the-influence (to give the matter a Heideggerian turn) with a vengeance. For whatever the particular terms in which it is couched, Baudelaire's indictment of Rousseau (whose *Reveries* Baudelaire acknowledged as a precursor to his own late work),[6] spectacularly breaches the division between intoxication by writing and intoxication by drugs that otherwise seems so decisive for Baudelaire's argument. The implications of this gesture are far reaching, for they identify as internal to the activity of writing itself the demonic threat Baudelaire finds embodied in drugs and indicate—not so surprisingly, after all—both a profound split in Baudelaire's attitude toward what Butor calls "cette drogue absolue qu'est la poésie" and, more important, a breaking up of the closed logic that subsumes poetry within the self-affecting production by means of language of a transcendent state of mind and thereby establishes the poet's autonomy vis-à-vis the reader.[7]

If this reading of Baudelaire's indictment of Rousseau is correct, it considerably vitiates the interest of *Les Paradis artificiels* as doctrinal statement, other than as a glaring instance of an aesthetic ideology riven by contradiction. At the same time, however, it opens up the possibility for reading the work not as statement, but as the conflict-driven elaboration of a writing practice, one intimately embattled with the very tendencies to poetic idealization that Baudelaire's manifest argument promotes. Some time ago Robert Guiette suggested in a brief essay titled "Des 'Paradis artificiels' aux 'Petits Poëmes en prose'" that the writing of *Les Paradis artificiels* should be looked at in the context of the stylistic shift that led Baudelaire from the classical versification of *Les Fleurs du mal* to the prose poetry of *Le Spleen de Paris*.[8] Certainly the dates of composition lend themselves to this argument, since both parts of *Les Paradis artificiels* ("Le Poème du hachisch" and Baudelaire's digest of De Quincey's *Confessions of an English Opium Eater* and *Suspiria de Profundis*) were written soon after the compilation of the 1857 *Fleurs du mal* and before the composition of most of the prose poems. The title too of "Le Poème du hachisch" distributes the metaphorical reference of "le poème" between the subject matter of the text, hashish, and its mode, the prose essay. And obviously De Quincey's writings on opium would not have engaged Baudelaire to the extent they did were it not for their experimental prose.[9] Notwithstanding these circumstances, which it requires some effort to overlook if one is familiar with the terrain, Guiette's suggestion has for the most part gone unexplored, and *Les Paradis artificiels* has been read, to the extent that it has been studied at all, largely for its pharmacological, doctrinal, or (encrypted) autobiographical interest (with the notable exception of the essay by Lyu referred to above).

In what follows, I pursue Guiette's idea, in the context of the other issues taken up in this study, by reflecting on how *Les Paradis artificiels* might participate in the development of the difficult, even rebarbative, writing practice that is Baudelaire's prose poetry. More specifically, I will ask how and why the elaboration of a certain theme—that of drugs and drugged experience—might have subserved such a formal development, bearing in mind Paul de Man's suggestive methodological notation: "We look for the delicate area where the thematic, semantic field and the rhetorical structures begin to interfere with each other, begin to engage each other" (*Romanticism and Contemporary Criticism*, 200n).

ONE WAY of entering into this question is to look more closely at the connection between the subject of drugs and the rhetoric of demonization or "satanism" that Flaubert found unsettling. Consider to begin with the following passage, surely one of those Flaubert took exception to, and which indeed anticipates objections to the "excessiveness" of its language:

> Qu'on prenne, si l'on veut, cette forme de langage pour une métaphore excessive, j'avouerai que les poisons excitants me semblent non seulement un des plus terribles et des plus sûrs moyens dont dispose l'Esprit des Ténèbres pour enrôler et asservir la déplorable humanité, mais même une de ses incorporations les plus parfaits.

[Take, if you will, this form of language for an excessive metaphor, I confess that stimulating poisons seem to me not only one of the most terrible and certain means the Spirit of Darkness has at his disposal for enlisting and enslaving deplorable humanity, but even one of his most perfect incorporations.] (*Oeuvres complètes,* 1:428–29)

The sting of this passage is in its tail. Had Baudelaire limited himself to characterizing drugs as a tool of the Spirit of Darkness, he would indeed merely be giving expression to a pious sentiment. But their supplemental categorization as "une de ses incorporations les plus parfaits" (and this is clearly the expression he anticipates will be received as "going too far") is another matter. In theological terms, the idea of the drug as a satanic "incorporation," and thus as an antithetical mirror of the host as the body of Christ and of the Son as the incarnation of the Father, is Manichaean and heterodox to say the least. But in the end it is simply the intensely compressed figure of "incorporation" that strikes with transgressive force. For if "incorporation," to begin with, simply means "embodiment" (and it is to emphasize this dimension of meaning that Baudelaire specifically refers in this passage to a shapeless "Spirit of Darkness"), in this instance it harbors as its destiny another and further incorporation—that of being taken into the body.

To better appreciate how deeply this exorbitant dynamic of "incorporation" is involved in Baudelaire's conception of the satanic, it will help to first consider instances in which that connection is *not* mediated or crystallized by references to drugs per se. And this requires that we briefly consider the prominent role that figures of ingestion play throughout his writing. As readers of Baudelaire know well, words such as *boire, manger, enivrer,* and *respirer* recur in his poetry with obsessive frequency. Another indication of their importance is how often they figure in programmatic theoretical statements. The famous declaration from the 1859 salon is only one of many such instances:

Tout l'univers visible n'est qu'un magasin d'images et de signes auxquels l'imagination donnera une place et une valeur relative: c'est une espèce de pâture que l'imagination doit digérer et transformer.

[The visible universe is but a storehouse of images and signs to which the imagination will assign a place and a relative value: it is a kind of food that the imagination must digest and transform.] (2:627)

Significantly, one encounters a related formulation in the dedication to *Les Paradis artificiels*: "Le monde natural pénètre dans le spirituel, lui sert de pâture" [The natural world penetrates into the spiritual, serves it as food] (1:399). As both these examples indicate, typically these figures operate in Baudelaire's language not as one set of metaphors among others but as metaphors of metaphor, dense sites of linguistic involution.

The second line of the early sonnet "Parfum exotique," "Je respire l'odeur de ton sein chaleureux" [I breathe in the odor of your warm breast], offers an apposite instance from the poetry, since in addition to its literal meaning the verb "respirer" facilitates the metaphorical subsumption of the beloved's physical emanation within the poet's spiritual distension (a movement subliminally underwritten by the figure of the infant at the mother's breast). This underlying metaphorical pattern is even clearer in the final tercet:

> Pendant que le parfum des vert tamariniers,
> Qui circule dans l'air et m'enfle la narine,
> Se mêle dans mon âme au chant des mariniers.

> [While the perfume of the green tamarind trees,
> Which eddies in the air and flares my nostrils,
> Merges in my soul with the song of the mariners.]

"Qui . . . m'enfle la narine" in particular marks the process of incorporation as one of metaphorical transfer, since the dilated atmosphere is appropriated as a dilation of the subject's body. At the same time, the spiritual merging of the perfumed air with "le chant des mariniers" confirms the governing chain of sublimations: female body—emanation—inspiration—male lyric voice.

Baudelaire's figurations of the satanic typically involve an inversion of this incorporative pattern, an inversion that occurs when the incorporative subject transfers to itself the very quality of "incorporability" that characterizes its objects and is thus an extension of the process it inverts. We may take as an example apposite to "Parfum exotique" the first stanza of "La Déstruction":

> Sans cesse à mes côtés s'agite le Démon;
> Il nage autour de moi comme un air impalpable;
> Je l'avale et le sens qui brûle mon poumon
> Et l'emplit d'un désir éternel et coupable.

[Ceaselessly on all sides the Demon round me stirs;
He swims about me like an impalpable air;
I swallow him and feel him as he burns my lungs
And fills them with an eternal and guilty desire.]

The incorporation of the other is accompanied here by a reversal of consumer and consumed most clearly marked by the verb *brûler,* which represents the demon as an internal fire consuming the body: as the speaker consumes the demon, the demon consumes the speaker. The line from "L'Héautontimoroumenos" (a poem that shares with *Les Paradis artificiels* a dedication to the enigmatic "J.G.F." as well as its title, which is borrowed from De Quincey's lexicon), "Je suis de mon coeur le vampire," is another particularly economical version of this pattern: the identification of the subject with the object of desire is complete, with the difference between self and other displaced within the self as a difference between whole and part.

One last example may suffice to document how closely Baudelaire links the idea of the satanic or demonic to this chiasmic "perfecting" of incorporative metaphors. The passage is from the conclusion to a critical essay on Théodore de Banville:[10]

Je veux dire que l'art moderne a une tendance essentiellement démoniaque. Et il me semble que cette part infernale de l'homme que l'homme prend plaisir à s'expliquer à lui-même, augmente journellement, comme si le Diable s'amusait à la grossir par des procédés artificiels, à l'instar des engraisseurs, empâtant patiemment le genre humain dans ses bassecours pour se préparer une nourriture plus succulente.

[I mean that modern art has an essentially demoniacal tendency. And it seems to me that this infernal part of man, which man takes pleasure in explaining to himself, grows with each passing day, as though the Devil took delight in fattening it by artificial means, after the fashion of geese breeders, patiently feeding humankind in his farmyards so as to prepare for himself a more succulent dish.] (2:168)

*

Dans l'épaisseur liquide, tremblant au fond de la drogue, toute la pharmacie se réfléchissait, répétant l'abîme de son phantasme.
                    —DERRIDA, "La Pharmacie de Platon"

Tout cela ne vaut pas le poison qui découle
De tes yeux, de tes yeux verts,
Lacs où mon âme tremble et se voit à l'envers.

— BAUDELAIRE, "Le Poison"

The allusion in the Banville passage to "procédés artificiels" brings us back to the theme of *Les Paradis artificiels* and to the insistence with which Baudelaire identifies drugs as satanic embodiments. We can now see that the literalizing thrust of this identification, and by extension the *prosaicness* of Baudelaire's "Poème du hachisch," must be understood in the context of the more extended patterns of figuration they concretize. But in order to further understand the relation between literalization and incorporation—which may be another way of describing the relation between prose as a mode and drugs as the demetaphorized subject of this mode—one needs to take into consideration another metaphorical series implicated in the Banville passage.

The phrase "grossir par des procédés artificiels" calls up, of course, a picture of the devil fattening man by stuffing him with some sort of unnatural food or by some unnatural means, a reading invited by the barnyard tableau that illustrates it. But if we read the phrase in the context of the reflexive remarks that introduce it ("Et il me semble que cette part infernale de l'homme, que l'homme prend plaisir à s'expliquer à lui-même, augmente journellement") an optical rather than organic image suggests itself: that of the devil holding up to man or appearing before him as a magnifying lens or mirror. Furthermore, the subsequent image of the devil as a giant poultryman towering over the flocks of human geese in his farmyards ("bassecours") reinforces this association of the satanic with a self-magnifying anthropomorphism.

We need not demonstrate that a connection between the figure of Satan and images of self-magnification circulates in Baudelaire's writing. This connection and the moral considerations concerning vanity and pride on which it is stamped are common coin. What concerns us more nearly is that Baudelaire specifically uses the image of self-magnification in "Le Poème du hachisch" to explain the nature of the drug's effect. The most prominent instance of this use occurs at the beginning of the essay's third section, in the context of a distinction between two kinds of dreams occurring in sleep: "le rêve naturel," which reflects the personality of the dreamer, and "le rêve hiéroglyphique ... sans rapport ni connexion avec le caractère, la vie et les passions du dormeur" [the hieroglyphic dream ... without relation or connection to the character, the life, or the passions of the dreamer]:

Dans l'ivresse du hachisch ... [n]ous ne sortirons pas du rêve naturel. ... Le cerveau et l'organisme sur lesquels opère le hachisch donneront que leur phénomènes ordinaires, individuels, augmentés, il est vrai, quant au nombre et à l'energie, mais toujour fidèles à leur origine. L'homme n'échappera pas à la fatalité de son temperament physique et moral: le hachisch sera, pour les impressions et les pensées familières de l'homme, un miroir grossissant, mais un pur miroir.

[In hashish intoxication ... we do not depart from the natural dream. ... The brain and the organism on which hashish works its effects will yield only their ordinary, individual phenomena, augmented, it is true, in number and force, but always faithful to their origin. Man will not escape the fatality of his physical and moral temperament: hashish will be, for man's impressions and familiar thoughts, a magnifying mirror but a pure mirror.] (1:408–9)

One may well imagine that this metaphor of optical magnification (complete with technical references to polarization and the invocation of mathematical terminology) was more congenial to Flaubert's desire to read *Les Paradis artificiels* as a work of science, as making the subject of drugs an occasion for expanding its field of cognition, than the idiom of satanic incorporation considered above. But, the two lines of development are not separable, and the following passage in particular marks their convergence:

Voici la drogue sous vos yeux: un peu de confiture verte, gros comme une noix, singulièrement odorante, à ce point qu'elle soulève une certaine répulsion et des velléités de nausée, comme le ferait, du reste, toute odeur fine et même agréable, portée à son maximum de force et pour ainsi dire de densité. Qu'il me soit permis de remarquer, en passant, que cette proposition peut être inversée, et que le parfum le plus repugnant, le plus revoltant, deviendrait peut-être un plaisir, s'il était reduit a son minimum de quantité et d'expansion.—Voilà donc le bonheur! Il remplit la capacité d'une petite cuiller! Le bonheur avec toutes ses ivresses, toute ses folies, tous ses enfantillages! Vous pouvez avalez sans crainte; on n'en meurt pas.

[Here is the drug before your eyes: a little bit of green jam, the size of a nut, and odorous to the point that it stirs a certain repulsion and small waves of nausea, as would, for that matter, any fine and even agreeable odor carried to its maximum of force and so to speak of density. May I be permitted to note in passing that this proposition may be inverted, and that the most repugnant, the most revolting, smell would perhaps be a pleasure were it reduced to its minimum of quantity and expansion.—Here then is happiness! It fills the capacity of a small spoon; happiness with all its intoxications, its follies, its childishness! You may swallow without fear; one doesn't die from it.] (1:410)

This is the most important of several passages in "Le Poème du hachisch" that focus on a description of the drug as a physical object. Baudelaire situates this description at the intersection of the same rhetorical patterns we found at work in the previously quoted passage on modern art. But whereas that passage warns us of the fascinating power of art, as of a present danger, here Baudelaire ironically extends an invitation; the fascinating virtues of the drug are held in reserve as a possibility, while its actual presence provokes resistance. Although the passage is rich in implications for the reading of all of Baudelaire's work, my comments will be guided by the particular problems this chapter deals with.

First of all, we may observe that the description of the drug is framed as a direct address to the reader: "Voici la drogue sous vos yeux. . . .Vous pouvez avalez sans crainte." Since what is literally "under our eyes" is the page of the text we are reading, this rhetorical gesture solicits the illusion that the author is present speaking to us from the text in the same manner that we are present as readers before the text, as well as the illusion that the object the text refers to is itself present in the text. The text is thus intensely—with the emphasis on tensely—aimed at the desire for authorial voice and substantial reference. At the same time the passage deals with its theme from a number of different perspectives, each placing a different emphasis on the subject. It is concerned with the drug as a physical substance of a certain characteristic size, color, texture, odor, and so on ("un peu de confiture verte"), as an incorporable substance ("Vous pouvez avaler sans crainte; on n'en meurt pas"), as an intoxicating substance ("Voilà donc le bonheur!"), and as an absent object to which the text is in some relation of substitution.

These perspectives do not, however, simply collect or associate as attributes around a supporting substance or word. Rather, Baudelaire's description of hashish as a physical substance places it in a relation of *resistance* to the possibility of incorporation by describing it as a vomitive: "un peu de confiture verte, gros comme une noix, singulièrement odorante, à ce point qu'elle soulève une certain répulsion et des velléités de nausée." Similarly, considered as a substance, the drug is placed in an antithetical relation to its effect as a "miroir grossissant." Baudelaire speculates that its repulsiveness is due to its density, which is in an inverted relation to the attractive permeability of a dilated atmosphere. The dilation of a fragrant atmosphere implies, like the image of the magnifying mirror, an expanding sense of permeability between subject and object. It is not only that the drug is associated with the reduction rather than the expansion of an osmotic zone, but that the reduction also involves a reversal whereby the permeable zone becomes an impermeable object. The drug appears here situated at the dead center of a mise-en-abyme, in which the possibility of an infinite expansion is encrypted.[11] Thus where Baudelaire uses the language of drugs in the most literal manner possible, to refer to an identifiable substance having predictable effects rather than metaphorically to refer to something else that works like a drug, or metonymically to refer to the drug's effect, that language continues to inscribe a network of rhetorical transformations, but in the mode of resistance.

It is not then so much in order to write *about* poetry, as Butor proposes, that Baudelaire is led to compose his book on drugs, as to write *against* it— to write about what precisely resists metaphor by literalizing its fundamental operations. Baudelaire's is in many ways a remarkable case, since it was primarily with the acute self-consciousness of his own poetry that his work as a writer had to contend for survival. But the itinerary of that work compresses the history we have been tracing in these chapters, a history that moves through the sublimations of self-reflection toward the literalizing and imaginatively violent dynamics of incorporation they idealize.

WE MAY FIND a fitting emblem for the kind of work *Les Paradis artificiels* performs in "Haschisch in Marseilles," a late autobiographical essay by Baudelaire's best reader, Walter Benjamin. Just as Baudelaire's "Poème du hachisch" is written in direct dialogue with De Quincey's *Confessions of an English Opium Eater,* so does Benjamin's essay hark back directly to Baudelaire's. For the long clinical note that Benjamin cites in the epigraph to "Haschisch in Marseilles" concludes with the observation that "Die vorzüglichste Schilderung des Haschischrausches stammt von Baudelaire (Paradis artificiels)." ["The preeminent description of hashish intoxication comes from Baudelaire (Paradis artificiels)"] (*Illuminationen,* 344–45). This is a clear signal that Benjamin wrote his piece with Baudelaire's specifically in mind and that his "experiments" with hashish were deeply entangled with his writerly identifications.

One paragraph in particular, though it does not specifically refer to

Baudelaire, combines a reflection on hashish-induced trance states with a reflection on what Benjamin calls "prosaförmige Produktivität":

> Man müsste, um den Rätseln des Rauschglücks näher zu kommen, über den Ariadne-Faden nachdenken. Welche Lust in dem blossen Akt, einen Knäuel abzurollen. Und diese Lust ganz tief verwandt mit der Rauschlust wie mit der Schaffenslust. Wir gehen vorwärts; wir entdecken dabei aber nicht nur die Windungen Höhle, in die wir uns vorwagen, sonder geniessen dieses Entdeckerglück nur auf dem Grunde jener anderen rhythmischen Seligkeit, die da im Abspulen eines Knäuel besteht. Eine solche Gewissheit vom kunstreich gewundenen Knäuel, das wir abspulen—ist das nicht das Glück jeder, zumindest prosaförmigen, Produktivität? Und im Haschisch sind wir geniessende Prosawesen höchster Potenz.

> [One must, in order to get at the riddle of the happiness of intoxication, reflect on Ariadne's thread. What pleasure in the mere act of unrolling a skein. And this pleasure is deeply bound up with the pleasure of intoxicated states, as it is with the pleasure of making something. We go forward; we not only discover thereby the windings of the caves we venture into, however, but partake of this happiness of discovery only against the ground of that other rhythmical bliss, which consists in the reeling out of a skein. The certainty of an artfully wound skein, which we reel out—Is this not the happiness of all productivity, at least of all that is prosaic in form? And in hashish we are savoring prose beings to the highest power.] (349)

In beginning this chapter, I cited Flaubert's hailing of *Les Paradis artificiels* as "le commencement d'une science." Benjamin's reflection on Ariadne's thread is also concerned with the glory of discovery, or what he calls "Entdeckerglück," but only as it occasions the endless, repetitive playing out of the already known that is its precondition and ground. As a solution to the problem of the labyrinth, Ariadne's thread is prosaic because it practically and locally navigates a space that remains conceptually unmasterable, denying us a synchronic survey or picture of its solution. In the same way, the philosophical or scientific ambitions of *Les Paradis artificiels* are ultimately important, we have been arguing, only insofar as they generate a writing process which undoes them and outlives them.

CHAPTER

Nine

Conclusion (Tailpiece)

*I*n my introduction I juxtaposed the preamble to Rousseau's *Confessions* with a text some two hundred years older, Montaigne's notice "To the Reader," to throw into relief and thus open to analysis the rhetoric of interiority that Rousseau's writing decisively inaugurates. In ending, I want to measure the distance traveled in this book and say something more explicit about our own moment in relation to the history we have been exploring. To do so, I propose to jump forward another two centuries and briefly juxtapose an early episode from the *Confessions* with a recent and intimately comparable piece of writing by Eve Kosofsky Sedgwick. (I should state at the outset that I am not proposing that Sedgwick's piece is in any way directly based on Rousseau's narrative. On the contrary, their comparability is all the more striking if one assumes the absence of any direct connection. On the other hand, Sedgwick herself remarks in the course of her essay, "I am struck, as they say, by the presence of French in this story" ["A Poem Is Being Written," 183].)

In the ninth of his "Theses on the Philosophy of History," Walter Benjamin offers his now well known reading of Klee's painting *Angelus Novus* (itself perhaps inspired by Rilke's blind Angel, figure of pure inwardness). "His face is turned toward the past . . . ," Benjamin writes. "But a storm is blowing from Paradise"—the storm we call progress—and "unceasingly drives him into the future on which he turns his back" while the catastrophic wreckage of history accumulates at his feet. ("Er hat das Antlitz der Vergangenheit zugewendet. . . . Aber ein Sturm weht vom Paradiese her . . . Dieser Sturm treibt ihn unaufhaltsam in die Zukunft, der er den Rücken kehrt . . . Das, was wir den Fortschritt nennen, ist dieser Sturm" [*Illuminationen,* 272–73]). If the angel's gaze is fixated—not unlike that of the boy in Wordsworth's boat-stealing episode—on a center and origin from which it is being traumatically expelled, then its back—and Benjamin's own meditation may be said to turn Klee's painting over and write on its back—is turned out toward an open future. As will quickly emerge, I hope, reading Sedgwick together with Rousseau may reveal something about this *back side* of Romantic interiority, a back side that may be the side of its future.

Like much of the later writing I have been considering, the piece by Sedgwick I will be drawing on, "A Poem Is Being Written," is a richly wrought work of prose poetry, gathering up poems and parts of poem written over a period of years in a prose matrix of autobiographical recollection and critical reflection. That reflection begins in meditation on "the two most rhythmic things which happened" to her when she was a child, "poetry and spanking" (182), and moves toward consideration of "the narrative and epistemological misrecognitions that surround *the absence of a discourse*—a discourse, specifically, of female anal eroticism" (178).

The passage from *The Confessions* to which I will be relating "A Poem Is Being Written" is among the earliest in book 1 and in fact is identified by Rousseau himself as "le prémier pas et le plus pénible dans le labirinthe obscur et fangeux de mes confessions" [the first and most difficult step in the dark and miry maze of my confessions] (1:18; Cohen translation, 28). It in fact inaugurates the narrative portion of the "Ébauches des Confessions," Rousseau's preliminary drafts, and follows directly a sentence that was to expand into the judgment scene of the preamble: "Mais que chaque lecteur m'imite; qu'il rentre en lui-même comme j'ai fait, et qu'au fond de sa conscience il se dise, s'il l'ose: *je suis meilleur que ne fut cet homme-là*" [But let each reader imitate me; let him withdraw into himself as I have done, and let him from the depths of his conscience say, if he dare to: *I am better than that man was*] (*Oeuvres complètes*, 1:1155). The story has this threshold status specifically because it is about something ridiculous and shameful rather than criminal: "Ce n'est pas ce qui est criminel qui coûte le plus à dire, c'est ce qui est ridicule et honteux" [It is the ridiculous and shameful, not one's criminal actions, that it is hardest to confess] (1:1155). And what is ridiculous and shameful is in this instance Rousseau's abiding wish to be spanked by a woman, a wish largely unfulfilled in his maturity, "l'espèce de jouissance dont l'autre n'étoit pour moi que le dernier terme ne pouvant être usurpée par celui qui la désire, ni devinée par celle qui peut l'accorder" [it being impossible for the kind of pleasure I desired—to which the other kind is no more than a consummation—to be taken by him who wants it, or to be guessed at by the woman who could grant it (1:17; Cohen translation, 27)], but whose incipience he dates to a "châtiment d'enfant receu à huit ans par la main d'une fille de trente" [childhood punishment received at the age of eight at the hands of a woman of thirty] (1:15; 26).

I would note parenthetically that, insofar as it revolves around the shameful rather than the criminal, the passage exemplifies a different confessional model than that embodied in the "Marion" episode at the end of book 2, which does indeed focus on two criminal acts, theft and slander, and which is the central text in de Man's reading of the *Confessions* in "Excuses." In that essay de Man moves from a reading of the Marion episode in terms of "the structure of desire as possession" to a reading in terms of "the structure of desire as exposure" and comments in passing, "What Rousseau really wanted is neither the ribbon nor Marion, but the public scene of exposure which he actually gets" (*Allegories of Reading*, 285). The distinction between a transgressive desire to possess and a transgressive desire to expose correlates very closely with Rousseau's distinction between what is "criminal" and what is "shameful and ridiculous." Having analyzed the former distinction, however, de Man reinscribes the movement of exposure within the category of the criminal ("since the crime is exposure, the excuse consists in recapitulating the exposure in the guise of concealment" [*Allegories of Reading*, 286]) and then moves beyond any appeal to desire as motivating, and thus explaining, the scene to an account in which the unmotivated free play of the signifier becomes the precipitating factor. In my own reading, the dynamics of shame are in some sense "premotivational" and thus are less assimilable to the logic of guilt and reparation, on the one hand, while on the other hand overlapping with the (il)logic of the free play of the signifier.

The episode in question pertains to the period when Rousseau, at roughly the same age as Wordsworth and after his father's flight from Geneva in the wake of a quarrel with a politically well connected French army officer, first leaves home to board with a country minister and his sister, M. and Mlle Lambercier. Here is the central narrative:

Je puis dire ici que l'attente des réprimandes de Mlle Lambercier me donnoit moins d'allarme que la crainte de la chagriner.

   Cependant elle ne manquoit pas au besoin de sévérité, non plus que son frére: mais comme cette sévérité, presque toujours juste, n'étoit jamais emportée, je m'en affligeois et ne m'en mutinois point. J'étois plus fâché de déplaire que d'être puni, et le signe du mécontentement m'étoit plus cruel que la peine afflictive. Il est embarrassant de s'expliquer mieux, mais cependant il le faut. Qu'on changeroit de méthode avec la Jeunesse si l'on voyoit mieux les effets éloignés de celle qu'on employe toujours indistinctement et souvent indiscretement! La grande leçon qu'on peut tirer d'un éxemple aussi commun que funeste, me fait résoudre à le donner.

Comme Mlle Lambercier avoit pour nous l'affection d'une mère, elle en avoit aussi l'autorité, et la portoit quelquefois jusqu'à nous infliger la punition des enfans, quand nous l'avions méritée. Assez longtems elle s'en tint à la menace, et cette menace d'un châtiment tout nouveau pour moi me sembloit très effrayante; mais après l'execution, je la trouvai moins terrible à l'épreuve que l'attente ne l'avoit été, et ce qu'il y de plus bisarre est que ce châtiment m'affectionna davantage encore à celle qui me l'avoit imposé. Il falloit même toute la vérité de cette affection et toute ma douceur naturelle pour m'empêcher de chercher le retour du même traitement en le méritant: car j'avois trouvé dans la douleur, dans la honte même, un mélange de sensualité qui m'avoit laissé plus de desir que de crainte de l'éprouver derechef par la même main. Il est vrai que, comme il se meloit sans doute à cela quelque instinct précoce du séxe le même châtiment receu de son frere ne m'eut point du tout paru plaisant. Mais de l'humeur dont il étoit, cette substitution n'étoit guère à craindre, et si je m'abstenois de mériter la correction, c'étoit uniquement de peur de fâcher Mlle Lambercier; car tel est en moi l'empire de la bienveillance, et même de celle que les sens ont fait naître, qu'elle leur donna toujours la loi dans mon coeur.

Cette récidive que j'éloignois sans la craindre arriva sans qu'il y eut de ma faute, c'est à dire, de ma volonté, et j'en profitai, je puis dire, en sureté de conscience. Mais cette seconde fois fut aussi la derniére: car Mlle Lambercier s'étant sans doute apperçue à quelque signe que ce châtiment n'alloit pas à son but, déclara qu'elle y renonçoit et qu'il la fatigoit trop. Nous avions jusques là couché dans sa chambre, et même en hiver quelquefois dans son lit. Deux jours après on nous fit coucher dans une autre chambre, et j'eus désormais l'honneur dont je me serois bien passé d'être traité en grand garçon.

[But I may say now that the expectation of a scolding from Mlle Lambercier alarmed me less than the fear of annoying her.

Neither she nor her brother was lacking in severity when necessary. But as their severity was almost always just and never excessive, I took it to heart and never resented it. I was more upset at displeasing them, however, than at being punished; and a word of rebuke was more painful to me than a blow. It embarrasses me to be more explicit, but it is necessary nevertheless. How differently people would treat children if only they saw the eventual results of the indiscriminate, and often culpable, methods of punishment they employ! The magnitude of the lesson to be derived from so common and unfortunate a case as my own has resolved me to write it down.

Since Mlle Lambercier treated us with a mother's love, she had also a mother's authority, which she exercised sometimes by inflicting on us such childish chastisements as we had earned. For a long while she confined herself to threats, and the threat of a punishment entirely unknown to me frightened me sufficiently. But when in the end I was beaten I found the experience less dreadful in fact than in anticipation; and the very strange thing was that this punishment increased my affection for the inflicter. It required all the strength of my devotion and all my natural goodness to prevent my deliberately earning another beating: I had discovered in the shame and pain of the punishment an admixture of sensuality which had left me rather eager than otherwise for a repetition by the same hand. No doubt, there being some degree of precocious sexuality in all this, the same punishment at the hands of her brother would not have seemed pleasant at all. But he was of too kindly a disposition to be likely to take over this duty; and so, if I refrained from earning a fresh punishment, it was only out of fear of annoying Mlle Lambercier; so much am I swayed by kindness, even by kindness that is based on sensuality, that it has always prevailed with me over sensuality itself.

The next occasion, which I postponed, although not through fear, occurred through no fault of mine—that is to say I did not act deliberately. But I may say that I took advantage of it with an easy conscience. This second occasion, however, was also the last. For Mlle Lambercier had no doubt detected signs that this punishment was not having the desired effect. She announced, therefore, that she would abandon it, since she found it too exhausting. Hitherto we had always slept in her room, and sometimes, in winter, in her bed. Two days afterward we were made to sleep in another room, and henceforward I had the honour, willingly though I would have dispensed with it, of being treated as a big boy.] (1:14–15; 25–26)

Before turning to Sedgwick's piece, let us first consider this passage in the context of the relation between the preamble to the *Confessions* and Montaigne's notice to the reader from which we set out. The first thing we may note is that, notwithstanding the stated reluctance with which Rousseau enters into his subject ("It is embarrassing to be more explicit, but it is nevertheless necessary"), the entire passage is a bravura performance evincing a distinct *plaisir d'écriture*. Indeed. the feelings of embarrassment and painful compulsion that Rousseau as writer avers correspond precisely to the feelings that become sources of pleasure for the eight-year-old boy who is being spanked, just as in both cases—for the child and for the writer—the pleasure, shame, and pain are mixed up with the compulsion to expose oneself so that a lesson may be taught.

Like the final paragraph of the preamble to the *Confessions* that we looked at in the introduction, the current passage both narrates a scene of self-display (a scene here situated in the past, whereas in the preamble it is projected into a mythical future) and enacts one in the process of writing. To state the matter in slightly different terms: an exposure that happens through writing is in both cases mediated by the narration of a scene of self-exhibition.

Granted this similarity, the relation between the two passages is by no means straightforward. Consider, for example, the justification with which Rousseau introduces the Mlle Lambercier story: "The magnitude of the lesson to be derived from so common and unfortunate a case as my own has resolved me to write it down." Whether one buys this didactic motive or not, it is distinctly supplemental to and potentially at variance with the principle of truth telling enunciated in the preamble: "I have spoken of the good and the bad with the same frankness." The introduction of this supplemental motive is only one index of the way the later passage, rather than simply beginning to implement the project announced in the preamble, turns the sublime rectitude of the opening inside out. Turning back to Montaigne, we can see that a different set of structuring oppositions is at work between the two writers than that between the body's surface and its interior. Considered in relation to Montaigne's figure of veiled nudity, what the Mlle Lambercier story offers us is a shift from front to back that is also a shift from high—or at least from the upright—to low and that performs the violation of decorum Montaigne's text hints at but claims to restrain itself from. In doing so it makes clearer the way Rousseau's appeal to a transcendent interiority disguises, at the same time that it promotes, his appropriation of the space of public self-exhibition as one of a common singularity.

In considering this episode, I have focused principally on the question of exposure and neglected other constitutive elements in the scenario, in particular the exercise of physical violence and the gendering of roles ("No doubt, there being some degree of precocious sexuality in all this, the same punishment at the hands of her brother would not have seemed pleasant at all"). In turning now to Sedgwick's essay, we may note that the portion I am principally concerned with, the section on "poetry and spanking," is characterized by Sedgwick herself as "relatively ungendered," and indeed in the narrative that she offers generational difference seems to play a far more organizing role than sexual difference: brothers and sisters alike, it seems, get spanked by fathers and mothers alike. But the title of Sedgwick's next book, the Silvan Tomkins reader *Shame and Its Sisters,* leads one to suspect that the "spankee" in this scenario is preeminently a sister, and if this is so then a more structured contrast emerges from the comparison with Rousseau. For in the latter the child's pleasure in subverting structures of authority is bound up with the possibility of a woman's striking a man. Consider now this central passage from "A Poem Is Being Written":

> Or maybe we should go back a bit. When I was a child the two most rhythmic things that happened to me were spanking and poetry. Not that I got spanked much: my big sister and I and our little brother were good and well-loved children and were not abused children, and it matters that this narrative is about an attentive, emotionally and intellectually generous matrix of nurturance and pedagogy. Still at times certainly, at the most memorable moments of our childlives (except that we barely remember them), suddenly within the quiet and agreeable space of the Biedermeyer family culture of upwardly mobile assimilated Jews in the 1950s there would constitute itself another, breath-holding space, a small temporary visible and glamorizing theater around the immobilized and involuntarily displayed lower body of a child. Of one of us. Not only shame itself, the forbidden, compulsory, and now too late longing to be excused from the eyes of others, which—or the forestalling or denial of which—was and maybe still is the wellspring of my own most characteristic motivations, was centered in this movable theater, but other plummier things as well. Wasn't it, after all, only the fat, innocent, and, at least in me, rankly profuse *exhibitionism* of an unpunished child that could lend this being compulsorily exhibited its peculiarly rich and lasting fetor of mortification? A primal hunger to be seen was certainly not undone in these punitive moments, but only made inseparable from the paralysis of my own rage and the potency and bland denial of my parents' rage; from the tensely not uncontrolled, repressed and repressive (and yet how speaking) rhythm of blows, or beats; from the tableau itself. (182–83)

This remarkable passage is systematically organized as a series of embedded gestures of discovery and exhibition, each the ground or frame of the one that follows, and each more pulsating with the flux of tension and discharge than the one before. First the novelistic delineation of a "quiet and agreeable" family space with its undercurrent of "upward mobility"; then within this quotidian space, and pertaining to a different temporality, the "breathholding" (thus time-stopping and "breathtaking") appearance of a "small temporary visible and glamorizing theater" itself framing "the immobilized and involuntarily displayed lower body of a child"; then the discovery of the child's "primal hunger to be seen," seasoned with the "fetor of mortification," and bonded, in what is the most knotted section of the paragraph, to the immobilizing rage of both parent and child; and finally the "action" that is played out in this immensely concentrated scene: "the tensely not uncontrolled, repressed and repressive (and yet how speaking) rhythm of blows, or beats."

I call attention to this progression (and this gesture of emphasis is scarcely more than a paraphrase of the passage itself, so heightened is its rhetorical self-consciousness) first of all to suggest its affinity with the essay's introductory paragraph, and its spiraling movement of display and correction. Thus Sedgwick begins with the statement, "This essay was written late: twenty-seven years late, to the extent that it represents a claim for respectful attention to the intellectual and artistic life of a nine-year-old child, Eve Kosofsky." But no sooner is this corrective claim articulated than it gives rise to new correction and more tensely charged self-dramatizations:

> What comes late, here, is then not her claim itself, which both deserves and was denied respect *because of its very commonplaceness,* but the rhetorical ground on which alone it can be made audible, which is unfortunately and misleadingly the ground of exception. She is allowed to speak, or I to speak of her, only here in the space of professional success and of hyperconscious virtuosity, conscious not least of the unusually narrow stylistic demands that hedge about any language that treats one's own past.

In its extended opening call for "respectful attention" to the writer's past, in the publicness of the arena within which that call is issued, in its vibratory logic of singularity whereby the commonplace and the exceptional constantly exchange places, the opening paragraph of Sedgwick's essay also provides a remarkably lucid analysis of the rhetorical dynamics of Rousseau's

Confessions, considered in its relation to Montaigne's *Essais,* as discussed above. The affinity is all the more striking given the similarity of the childhood memories to which each in its own way ascribes such importance and reminds us that the discursive economy of Romanticism has yet to exhaust its resources and power to disturb our settled habits of thought.

Of course Sedgwick's essay and Rousseau's autobiography also differ in ways so multiple and obvious that it would be an empty exercise indeed to begin to detail them. The question remains, however, whether certain of these differences may not carry special historical weight. I believe they do. The first of these is identified by Sedgwick herself, for as she clearly states, one project of her essay is to forge, or at least to analyze the effects of the absence of, a "discourse of female anal eroticism." This may seem like a highly specialized project, and it certainly is in many ways: no one would confuse it with building a gleaming city on a hill. But the power and prescience of Sedgwick's work has always involved identifying a specific and seemingly narrow area of investigation and then demonstrating how that place furnishes a point of cultural leverage and opening for fresh thought in which all manner of people might have a stake. The present case is no different.

Reading this project in its relation to Rousseau's, which itself must be read in relation to Montaigne's, I propose the following, admittedly schematic analysis: Sedgwick permits the dynamics of subversive self-exposure to be thematized as such and openly and aggressively pursued, thus rendering explicit tendencies that are at work in Rousseau but are not fully avowed. But what makes this possible is the introduction of another set of oppositions as instruments of analysis, namely those of gender. At the same time, one is led to ask whether the idiom of gendered difference, like that between the "inner" and the "outer," may not be stabilizing with respect to the widely oscillating dramas associated with an anal erotics. Certainly this is suggested by the direction of Sedgwick's own work, in which the question of shame has come increasingly to the fore and the problem of sexualities, in all their perverse multiplicity and singularity, has tended to displace the problem of gender. And this would leave as a new question for study an understanding of the relation between the aspects of orality we have been concerned with and these scandalous energies of queer performance.

Appendix A

Montaigne's Notice "Au Lecteur"

C'est ici un livre de bonne foy, lecteur. Il t'advertit dès l'entrée, que je ne m'y suis proposé aucune fin, que domestique et privée. Je n'y ay eu nulle consideration de ton service, ny de ma gloire. Mes forces ne sont pas capables d'un tel dessein. Je l'ay voué à la commodité particuliere de mes parens et amis: à ce que m'ayant perdu (ce qu'ils ont à faire bien tost) ils y puissent retrouver aucuns traits de mes conditions et humeurs, et que par ce moyen ils nourrisent plus entiere et plus vifve la connoissance qu'ils ont eu de moy. Si c'eust esté pour rechercher la faveur du monde, je me fusse mieux parè et me presenterois en une marche estudiée. Je veus qu'on m'y voie en ma façon simple, naturelle et ordinaire, sans contantion et artifice: car c'est moy que je peins. Mes defauts s'y liront au vif, et ma forme naïfve, autant que la reverence publique me l'a permis. Que si j'eusse esté entre ces nations qu'on dict vivre encore sous la douce liberté des premieres loix de nature, je t'asseure que je m'y fusse très-volontiers peint tout entier, et tout nud. Ainsi, lecteur, je suis moy-mesmes la matiere de mon livre: ce n'est pas raison que tu employes ton loisir en un subject si frivole et si vain. A Dieu donq; de Montaigne, ce premier de Mars mille cinq cens quatre ving.

[This book is open with you, reader. It lets you know from the outset that my end in writing it has been solely domestic and private. I have not been concerned with being of service to you or winning glory for myself. Such designs are beyond my powers. I have intended it for the particular use of my family and friends, so that having lost me (as soon they will), they may find in it some traces of my ways and dispositions and so nourish more completely and more vividly their recollection of me. Had I sought the world's favor, I would have donned finer array and assumed a more studied bearing. I want to be seen in my simple, natural, and ordinary guise, without straining or artifice: for it is myself that I paint. My faults will show through vividly and my native form, insofar as respect for the public has permitted. For were I among those nations that are said to still live under the sweet liberty of nature's first laws, I assure you that I would have readily painted myself in the altogether and quite naked. Thus, reader, I am myself the matter of my book: there is no sense in your spending your leisure on such a frivolous and vain subject. Adieu, then; from Montaigne, this first of March, one thousand five hundred and eighty.]

Appendix B

Rousseau's "Preamble" to the *Confessions*

Je forme une entreprise qui n'eut jamais d'éxemple, et dont l'exécution n'aura point d'imitateur. Je veux montrer à mes semblables un homme dans toute la vérité de la nature; et cet homme, ce sera moi.

Moi seul. Je sens mon coeur et je connois les hommes. Je ne suis fait comme aucun de ceux que j'ai vus; j'ose croire n'être fait comme aucun de ceux qui existent. Si je ne vaux pas mieux, au moins je suis autre. Si la nature a bien ou mal fait de briser le moule dans lequel elle m'a jetté, c'est ce dont on ne peut juger qu'après m'avoir lu.

Que la trompette du jugement dernier sonne quand elle voudra; je viendrai ce livre à la main me présenter devant le souverain juge. Je dirai hautement: voila ce que j'ai fait, ce que j'ai pensé, ce que je fus. J'ai dit le bien et le mal avec la même franchise. Je n'ai rien tu de mauvais, rien ajouté de bon, et s'il m'est arrivé d'employer quelque ornement indifférent, ce n'a jamais été que pour remplir un vide occasionné par mon défaut de mémoire; j'ai pu supposer vrai ce que je savois avoir pu l'être, jamais ce que je savois être faux. Je me suis montré tel que je fus, méprisable et vil quand je l'ai été, bon généreux, sublime, quand je l' ai été: j'ai dévoilé mon intérieur tel que tu l'as vu toi-même. Etre éternel, rassemble autour de moi l'innombrable foule de mes semblables: qu'ils écoutent mes confessions, qu'ils gémissent de mes indignités, qu'ils rougissent de mes miséres. Que chacun d'eux découvre à son tour son coeur aux pieds de ton trône avec la même sincérité; et puis qu'un seul te dise, s'il l'ose: *je fus meilleur que cet homme-là.*

[I plan an undertaking for which there is no example, and whose execution will have no imitator. I want to show my fellows a man in all the truth of his nature, and that man will be myself.

Myself alone. I feel what is in my heart, and I know men. I am not made like any I have seen, and I dare believe that I am not made like any who exist. If I am not better, at least I am other. Whether nature did well or ill to break the mold in which she cast me—this one may judge only after having read me.

Let the trumpet of the last judgment sound when it will. I will come, this book in hand, to present myself before the sovereign judge. I will say for all to hear: Here is what I have done, what I have said, what I was. I have spoken of the good and the bad with the same frankness. I have concealed nothing bad, added nothing good, and if it happened that occasionally I employed some inconsequential embellishment, this was only to make up for gaps occasioned by lapses of memory. I may have supposed to be true what I knew might be so, never what I knew to be false. I have shown myself as I was, despicable and vile when I was, good, generous, sublime when I was: I have unveiled my interior as you yourself have seen it. Eternal Being, gather round me the innumerable crowd of my fellows: let them listen to my confessions, let them bewail my unworthinesses, let them blush in shame at my miseries; let each of them uncover his heart at the feet of your throne with the same sincerity, and then let a single one say to you, if he dares: *I was better than that man.*]

Appendix C

The "Boat-Stealing" Episode
from Wordsworth's *Prelude*

One evening—surely I was led by her—
I went alone into a shepherd's boat,
A skiff that to a willow tree was tied
Within a rocky cave, its usual home.
'Twas by the shores of Patterdale, a vale
Wherein I was a stranger, thither come
A schoolboy traveller, at the holidays.
Forth rambled from the village inn alone,
No sooner had I sight of this small skiff,
Discovered thus by unexpected chance,
Than I unloosed her tether and embarked.
The moon was up, the lake was shining clear
Among the hoary mountains; from the shore
I pushed, and struck the oars and struck again
In cadence, and my little boat moved on
Even like a man who walks with stately step
Though bent on speed. It was an act of stealth
And troubled pleasure. Nor without the voice
Of mountain-echoes did my boat move on,
Leaving behind her still on either side
Small circles glittering idly in the moon,
Until they melted all into one track
Of sparkling light. A rocky steep uprose
Above the cavern of the willow-tree,
And now, as suited one who proudly rowed
With his best skill, I fixed a steady view

Upon the top of that same craggy ridge,
The bound of the horizon—for behind
Was nothing but the stars and the grey sky.
She was an elfin pinnace; lustily
I dipped my oars into the silent lake,
And as I rose upon the stroke my boat
Went heaving through the water, like a swan—
When from behind that craggy steep, till then
The bound of the horizon, a huge cliff
Rose up between me and the stars, and still,
With measured motion, like a living thing,
Strode after me. With trembling hands I turned,
And through the silent water stole my way
Back to the cavern of the willow-tree.
There, in her mooring-place, I left my bark,
And, through the meadows homeward went, with grave
And serious thoughts; and after I had seen
That spectacle, for many days, my brain
Worked with a dim and undetermined sense
Of unknown modes of being; in my thoughts
There was a darkness—call it solitude,
Or blank desertion—no familiar shapes
Of hourly objects, images of trees,
Of sea or sky, no colours of green fields;
But huge and mighty forms that do not live
Like living men moved slowly through my mind
By day and were the trouble of my dreams.

The Prelude (1805), 372–426

Notes

One | Interface

1. An example for our times: "You may not have this experience, but I think a lot of people have the experience that you know something but to be able to internalize it and do it is different than knowing it." Newt Gingrich explaining the title of his book, *Lessons Learned the Hard Way,* to Ted Koppel on *Nightline,* 2 April 1998.

2. Cf. Paul de Man's remark that "Hegel is indeed, from the relatively early *Phenomenology* to the late *Aesthetics,* prominently the theoretician of internalization, of *Erinnerung* as the ground of the aesthetic as well as of the historical consciousness" (*Aesthetic Ideology* 100).

3. Although enough work in contemporary literary studies (broadly construed) is informed by psychoanalytic discussions of internalization that one may speak of something like an emergent field of inquiry, the terrain is by no means easily mapped, nor has there been any explicit consideration of the relation between the rhetorical and psychoanalytic uses of the term "internalization." Speaking very generally, one may identify three often convergent lines of exploration, and this book has affinities with each.

The first tends to focus on Freud's analysis of identification with the lost object in "Mourning and Melancholia," since the pattern of incorporation he proposes there may be related to processes of representation generally and poetic representation in particular. Derrida's reading of Abraham and Torok's work in "Fors" plays a crucial mediating role here, though Julia Kristeva's equally influential work on abjection (first in *Pouvoirs de l'horreur*) and the melancholic imaginary (in *Soleil noir*) takes its own route toward related areas. A relatively recent example of work in this line would be Anselm Haverkampf's *Leaves of Mourning* (*Laub voll Trauer*).

A second and more specifically American tendency has engaged critically with psychoanalytic theories of internalization under the aegis of cultural studies or queer theory, and with the purpose of analyzing the ideological origins and functions of those theories. Judith Butler's *Gender Trouble,* which also participates in the current of work on melancholia and representation, may be seen as initially channeling a portion of that current in this direction, while Diana Fuss's *Identification Papers* would be the most developed instance of such work and Elizabeth Mayes's essay "The Fantasy of Internalization in the Theoretical Imaginary" perhaps the most recent. (In her book, Fuss broadly refers to identification as "a process defined as the internalization of the other" [4], although she also rightly emphasizes the confusion surrounding the concept. In the opening pages of chapter 4 I briefly discuss Fuss's critique of the Freudian distinction between "object choice" and "identification" and the controversy it sparked.)

Though less concerned with positioning itself in relation to Freud, Eve Kosofsky Sedgwick's *Epistemology of the Closet*, considered as an investigation of the history of modern interiority, bears an especially intimate relation to the current project, and I turn directly to her work in my conclusion.

Finally, in surveying this emergent "field" one should take into account the appearance in recent years of a fair amount of work on literature, drugs, and addiction, among which Richard Klein's *Cigarettes Are Sublime,* Avital Ronell's *Crack Wars,* and the recent volume of *Diacritics* on literature and addiction edited by Marc Redfield would be three of the more important instances.

4. The writings of the American psychoanalyst Roy Schafer bear striking witness to this felt obscurity. In 1968 Schafer published *Aspects of Internalization,* the first book-length attempt to sift and systematize psychoanalytic discussions of internalization. By 1972, however, in an article titled "Internalization: Process or Fantasy?" Schafer had come to the conclusion that the term "internalization" could be properly used only with reference to fantasies of incorporation; that all other processes that psychoanalysis described by spatial metaphors were better considered in terms of shifts between passivity and activity; and that the "spooky" psychoanalytic language of "introjection" tended to repeat rather than analyze primitive incorporative fantasies (Schafer, *New Language,* 36). (Readers of Abraham, Torok, and Derrida will be interested to see a debate about "fantasy" and "process," linked to an attempt to distinguish incorporation and introjection, surfacing in an American context largely innocent at the time of French psychoanalytic controversies.) By 1976 Schafer had written *A New Language for Psychoanalysis,* a book that seeks to purge psychoanalytic discourse of these "spooky" elements by replacing a language of "inner" and "outer" with a "new language" of "active" and "passive." For Meissner's response to Schafer, see "A Note on Internalization as Process" (1976) and "Methodological Critique of the Action Language in Psychoanalysis" (1979).

5. I do not claim any special originality for many aspects of the "model" of internalization proposed here. As I note above, Freud's own model of internalization is a bifurcated one, and recourse to language as that element that bridges discontinuities in a topological model of the psyche occurs throughout his writings and is developed systematically in his essay "The Unconscious" (most specifically in its concluding section, "Assessment of the Unconscious" [*Standard Edition,* 14:196–204]), among other places. Moreover, Meissner himself characterizes his exploration of internalization as one that "weaves itself" (*Internalization in Psychoanalysis,* xi) between "Kernberg's . . . psychology of object relations, in which the origins of the self are cast in terms of internalized object relations," and "Kohut's theory [which] casts the origins of the self in terms of internal vicissitudes of narcissism, along a developmental line almost separate from involvement with objects" (x). His claim that an understanding of internalization must take into account both "internalized object relations" and "the internal vicissitudes of narcissism" seems to me a more evolved and circumstantial version of my own claim that the notion of internalization articulates ideas of transfer and ideas of involution.

On the other hand, my emphasis on an element within this interweaving of "contingent articulation," connected with language and resistant to spatialization, is indebted most directly to Paul de Man's writing and teaching. Indeed, this book may within limits be understood as an attempt to graft a de Manian conception of rhetoric onto a psychoanalytic conception of internalization and vice versa, and thus as only one of many current efforts to bring psychoanalysis and deconstruction into closer relation with one another.

6. Symptomatically, it is the preposition "into" that condenses the ambiguity and richness of Bloom's formulation. Etymologically, "transposing into" suggests moving something across a boundary from a place without to a place within. But the latent musical metaphor suggests transposition from one key to another, a transformation for which there is no ready spatial analogy. Finally, and most important, the formulation implies relations of involution and condensation whose occurrence the spatial scheme may mark but can only reductively represent. For what Bloom has in mind in speaking of the poet's "own imaginative life" is not so much the poet's fantasies as the succession of the poet's writings interpreted and narrated as stages in a quest. The work that undertakes this narrative synthesis (and conceivably each of the poet's works may be understood as undertaking it, each time with a difference) will itself also be an episode in—and a temporally condensed recapitulation of—the narrative it relates.

7. Thus de Man, for example, while associating "the dialectics of internalization" with the "ideology of the symbol" and "the commonplaces of our own historical discourse on literature," defines the former in terms of a neat chiasmus: "the external manifestation of an ideal content which is itself an interiorized experience, the recollected emotion of a bygone perception" (*Aesthetic Ideology*, 100). But the symmetry of this formulation is not achieved without some violence, most notably in the substitution of "perception" for "emotion" in the allusion to Wordsworth's remarks on "emotion recollected in tranquillity."

8. As Cathy Caruth has noted, speaking in more general terms, "Our self-understanding, as articulated within psychoanalytic discourse, can be understood historically, in terms of the relation between psychoanalytic theory and the texts of an earlier period called Romanticism" ("Past Recognition," 44).

9. I discuss the connection between Freud and Nietzsche, which Walter Kaufmann remarks on in his translation of the *Genealogy of Morals* (84n), at slightly greater length in chapter 3. Here I would also note in passing Nietzsche's systematic elaboration of figures of ingestion to talk about psychic and symbolic processes, and in particular, his comment at the end of his preface to the *Genealogy* that "one thing is necessary above all if one is to practice reading as an *art* . . . —something for which one has almost to be a cow and in any case *not* a 'modern man': *rumination*" ("das Wiederkäuen"; literally "chewing over again" [Nietzsche, *Werke*, 2:770; Kaufmann translation, 23]).

The implication of figures of digestive assimilation in philosophical discussions of understanding is at least as old as Aristotle, who exemplifies his often cited, and almost always misunderstood, dictum that "art imitates nature" by reference to the relation between cooking and digestion: the art (*techne*) of cooking imitates (*mimetai*) and completes the natural process of digestion, the ultimate purpose of both being to render food assimilable. (The function Lévi-Strauss assigns in *The Raw and the Cooked* to the cooking of food as a primary way of marking of the distinction between nature and culture offers an interesting modern counterpart to Aristotle's analogizing.) Although Nietzsche's elaboration of a metaphoric of incorporation undoubtedly develops in relation to this very old tradition, it is probably via the Romantic dialectic of reflection and its attendant rhetoric of organic totalization (desublimated in Nietzsche's literalizing play on rumination) that Nietzsche inherits the topos. Thus, to cite one small but telling instance, his remarks on the art of reading and "das Wiederkäuen" cited above manifestly involve an allusion to a passage in Schopenhauer's 1818 preface to *The World as Will and Representation* in which he states that, given the organic unity of his thought and the linearity of exposition by book, "in order that the thought expounded may be fathomed, no advice can be given other than *to read the book twice,* and to do so the first time with much patience" (1:xiii; Schopenhauer's emphasis).

10. Indeed, schemas of internalization are as integral to the discourse of ideological critique as they are to histories of Romanticism. Cf. Marx's famous dictum in *The German Ideology:* "If in all ideology men and their circumstances appear upside-down as in a camera obscura, this phenomenon arises just as much from their historical life-process as the inversion of objects on the retina does from their physical life-process" (47). In this passage, the idealism that inverts the operative relations between consciousness and its material conditions is at once a turning upside down and a movement from outside to inside. We will encounter this pattern again.

11. A related argument, far more grounded than my own in a detailed analysis of the changing political economy of the era and not specifically concerned with the problem of internalization, may be found in Jerome Christensen's *Lord Byron's Strength,* which I draw on in chapter 7.

12. Rousseau's declaration of intent, for example: "Je veux montrer à mes semblables un homme dans toute la vérité de la nature; et cet homme, ce sera moi" [I want to show my fellows a man in all the truth of nature; and this man will be myself] (*Oeuvres complètes,* 1:5), is recognizably a transformation of Montaigne's more modest proposition: "Je veus qu'on m'y voie en ma façon simple, naturelle et ordinaire, sans contantion et artifice: car c'est moy que je peins" [I want to be seen in my simple, natural, and ordinary fashion, without contention or artifice: for it's myself that I paint] (*Oeuvres complètes,* 9). In draft material for the opening of the *Confessions,* Montaigne figures explicitly as the master of those who lie in telling the truth, the personification (and projection), in effect, of a deep-seated epistemological quandary: "Les plus sincères sont vrais tout au plus dans ce qu'ils disent, mais ils mentent par leurs réticences, et ce qu'ils taisent change tellement ce qu'il feignent d'avouer, qu'en ne disant qu'une partie de la vérité il ne disent rien. Je mets Montaigne à la tête de ces faux sincères qui veulent tromper en disant vrai" [The most sincere are truthful at most in what they say, but they lie in what they hold back; and what they do not say so changes

what they seem to admit to that in saying but a part of the truth they say nothing. I place Montaigne at the head of these false paragons of sincerity who aim to deceive through speaking truly] (1:1149–50).

13. That the contentious allusion to Montaigne, though implicit, would be instantly recognizable to Rousseau's readership involves a further dimension of the dynamics of internalization: its relation to the secret or, to use Abraham and Torok's term, the crypt. I take up the "inner" relation between concealment and internalization most directly in chapters 3 and 4.

14. One may also note that while Montaigne's figure elaborates the preceding metaphor of self-portraiture ("c'est moy que je peins"), it moves toward an identification of his writing with literal self-exhibition, an ambiguity that receives its most compressed expression in the ensuing claim, "je suis moy-mesmes la matiere de mon livre," where "matiere" may be read as "subject matter," but more radically and more in keeping with the figural drift of the passage as the "matter" out of which the book is made. The writer's embodiment in his text thus becomes coextensive with his vanishing, a relationship underscored by the "Adieu" that directly follows the claim just quoted and in turn yields to a testamentary dating and signing.

15. This is, of course, how Freud characterizes the position of the ego in the topological model of the psyche presented in *Beyond the Pleasure Principle* and *The Ego and the Id,* a model for which the groundwork is established in numerous earlier writings going back to the *Project for a Scientific Psychology.* A variation on the figure of the double or divided face also appears in Rousseau's comments on Montaigne, when he writes, "Montaigne se peint ressemblant mais de profil. Qui sait si quelque balafre à la joue ou un oeil crêvé du côté qu'il nous a caché, n'eut pas totalement changé sa physionomie" [Montaigne paints his likeness, but in profile. Who knows whether some scar on his cheek or a blinded eye on the side he hides from us would not have totally changed his physiognomy] (*Oeuvres complètes,* 1:1150). Here the opposition is not between being turned outward and being turned inward but between being turned toward and being turned away from the other. We can see how this latter contrast might easily transmute into the former, but we can also see how such a shift produces a more abstract and unified picture of the "outer."

16. Consider, for example, the following untitled note accompanying the Geneva manuscript and first published in 1850 (Rousseau, *Oeuvres complètes,* 1:1230 n. 3):

Qui que vous soyez que ma destinée ou ma confiance ont fait l'arbitre du sort de ce cahier, je vous conjure par mes malheurs, par vos entrailles, et au nom de toute l'espèce humaine de ne pas anéantir un ouvrage unique et utile, lequel peut servir de premiere pièce de comparaison pour l'étude des hommes, qui certainement est encore à commencer, et de ne pas ôter à l'honneur de ma mémoire *le seul monument sur de mon caractère qui n'ait pas été défiguré par mes ennemis* (1:3; my emphasis).

[Whoever you may be whom either destiny or my trust has made the arbiter of the fate of this notebook, I beseech you by my misfortunes, by your entrails, and in the name of all humankind not to annihilate a unique and useful work, one that might serve as the first piece for comparison in the study of men, which is certainly yet to begin, and not to deprive the honor of my memory of *the only secure monument of my character that has not been disfigured by my enemies.*]

17. I offer this as more than a casual comparison. The word "spots" obviously suggests, in addition to the idea of a place, in particular a picturesque "spot," the image of a discrete circular mark—a kind of protoperiod. But beyond these visual associations, the word "spots" is also recognizably an anagram—in fact, a palindrome—of "stops," and "stops of time" may well make us think on a sublime scale of the sun standing still, but on a more prosaic level of the full stop marking the end of a sentence, that is, the period. Furthermore, the polysemous, anagrammatic way the word "spots" functions in the context of these lines establishes the word not only as signifying a spatial concentration but as itself a site of linguistic *condensation,* and thus as calling attention to its own materiality as mark.

18. To properly situate my brief remarks on this passage in relation to those of other recent commentators would require a long detour. But I direct readers' attention in particular to Cathy Caruth's analysis in "Past Recognition: Narrative Origins in Wordsworth and Freud" of the way Wordsworth's rendering of the scene conjoins the "prop" of the maternal breast with the specular exchange of gazes between mother and infant, and to Neil Hertz's extremely nuanced discussion in "Lurid Figures" of the way Paul de Man's reading of the passage suppresses consideration of a possible link between "seeing and sucking" (97).

Two | Romanticism and the Internalization of Scripture

1. Cf. Paul de Man's observation in "Semiology and Rhetoric" that "in France, a semiology of literature comes about as the outcome of the long-deferred but all the more explosive encounter of the nimble French literary mind with the category of form" (*Allegories of Reading,* 6).

2. Spivak translates this phrase as "a modification well within the platonic schema," but the French is more equivocal here than this translation suggests. Grammatically, the ambiguity turns on the function of the preposition *de.* Is it attached to *modification,* in which case something like the translation I have offered, "a wholly interior modification of the Platonic schema," would be in order; or is it attached to the adjective *intérieur* (by analogy with the locution *à l'intérieur de*—although strictly speaking the preposition that accompanies *intérieur* when it functions adjectivally is *à* rather than *de*), in which case Spivak's translation would be more accurate? The ambiguity cannot be resolved through an appeal to context, since the argument that precedes the quoted phrase (and from which I draw my other citations) largely supports the former reading, whereas the sentences that immediately follow lend more support to the latter. The equivocation corresponds to a more global difficulty in the narrative and conceptual structure of *De la grammatologie* to which Derrida himself repeatedly calls attention.

Consider, for example, his claim at the end of part 1 that "tous les concepts proposés jusqu'ici pour penser l'articulation d'un discours et d'une totalité historique sont pris dans la clôture metaphysique que nous questionnons ici" [all the concepts proposed up to this point for thinking the articulation of a discourse and a historical totality are caught in the metaphysical closure we are questioning here] (148). Thus the questions being raised here about the historicizing rhetoric of *De la grammatologie* are questions that Derrida explicitly solicits.

3. Note that Dante uses the term "allegorical" to refer to all the senses of the Bible that are not literal, as well as to a specific modality of sense. It is the latter that is at issue here, though its centrality to the entire system of interpretation is suggested by the ambiguity of the term.

4. For a thoughtful and detailed reading of the poem along these lines see Stuart M. Sperry's "Tragic Irony: 'The Fall of Hyperion.'"

5. See Miriam Allott's annotations in her edition of the collected poems.

6. Keats's work offers, of course, many instances of this kind of imaginative projection. Compare, for example, the opening stanza of the "Ode to Psyche."

7. For an extended exemplification of this claim, see my reading of "Nutting" in chapter 5.

8. I have in mind here not only Kafka's parable, but also Frank Kermode's discussion of that parable in the introduction to *The Genesis of Secrecy*, which may be seen as studying the institutional regulation of textual inscrutability.

9. Geoffrey Hartman's "'Timely Utterance' Once More" (reprinted in *The Unremarkable Wordsworth*) is an important exception to these claims. Although Hartman's comments on "My Heart Leaps Up" are contained within a reading of the "Immortality Ode," they stress the paradigmatic status of the shorter lyric and establish it as a focus of interpretive attention.

10. See Paul de Man's well-known discussion of the relation between allegory and symbol in Romantic writing in "The Rhetoric of Temporality" (reprinted in the second edition of *Blindness and Insight*). A later essay concerned with related issues is de Man's "Sign and Symbol in Hegel's Aesthetics" (reprinted in *Aesthetic Ideology*).

11. Abrams is the editor specifically responsible for the Romantic period as well as the general editor of the anthology.

12. On subjective universality in Kant's analysis of the form of aesthetic judgment, see Stanley Cavell's "Two Problems of Aesthetics" in *Must We Mean What We Say?*

13. The remark is part of a longer argument emphasizing the instability, in Wordsworth, of the pastoral "ideal of harmony or correspondence." See as well Hartman's "Poetics of Prophecy," also reprinted in *The Unremarkable Wordsworth,* in which he discusses how, in Wordsworth's writing, "The poet as reader is shown to have discovered from within himself, and so recreated, a scripture text" (178). At the same time, Hartman relates this discovery to the poet's "entanglement in a certain order of sensations" (165) that involves the violent "harmonizing" of conflicting desires and allegiances.

14. For a much more extended consideration of the complex temporality of promising in Wordsworth, see Cathy Caruth's "'Unknown Causes': Poetic Effects."

Three | Monster Feedback

1. This problem is, of course, hardly foreign to psychoanalysis, having bedeviled it from the time Freud abandoned his seduction theory in favor of a fantasy theory of the origins of childhood trauma. But as contemporary controversies bear witness, the theoretical terms of the psychoanalytic debate have not progressed much beyond the state in which Freud left them. For genuine conceptual inquiries into the epistemology of autobiographical narrative, one has to turn to literary theory and philosophy. And even there one must distinguish between a deconstructive approach to the problem, particularly as elaborated by Paul de Man in essays such as "Autobiography as Self-Defacement" (reprinted in *The Rhetoric of Romanticism*) and the final chapter of *Allegories of Reading* ("Excuses"), and an ordinary language approach (not necessarily to autobiography as such but to various kinds of first-person claims) coming out of Wittgenstein's *Philosophical Investigations* and pursued in Stanley Cavell's work on skepticism, including most recently *A Pitch of Philosophy: Autobiographical Exercises.*

2. The modulation is in fact ungrammatical, since the apostrophized "thou" is not part of the closing "we," though the rhetorical force of the initial act of address carries over to that convocation. "Mild" anacoluthona of this kind are remarkably frequent in Wordsworth, though I am not aware that they have been the subject of extended study.

3. Freud's claim that he had never studied Nietzsche is widely known and almost as widely doubted. For a detailed consideration of the question, see Lehrer, *Nietzsche's Presence.*

4. With Richard Onorato's interpretation in *The Character of the Poet* (268–74) being the best known and David Collings's in *Wordsworthian Errancies,* which finds encoded in the phrase "upreared its head" a phantasm of anal rape by the father, perhaps the most recent and daring (135–39). In partial support of the latter reading, see my comments below on the passage's relation to "Lycidas."

5. The "ins and outs" of Klein's account are far more complicated than this brief, and no doubt tendentious, summary suggests. Nonetheless it is clear that as a whole the process she is concerned with tends toward a guilt-ridden incorporation of the object.

6. See the manuscript drafts and fragments in the Norton *Prelude* and the editors' note on these latter lines (1n).

7. Significantly, Wordsworth deleted the lines in question from later versions of the episode.

8. Economic in the most literal sense. In contrast with the nest-robbing exploit that follows, for example, the snaring of woodcocks was a source of livelihood, with the game birds brought to market for transportation to London (Norton edition 2n).

9. We may note in passing the close similarity between Wordsworth's recollection

of himself setting forth "my shoulders all with springes hung" and his "sallying forth / a huge wallet o'er my shoulder hung" at the opening of "Nutting." I discuss the lines from "Nutting" in chapter 5.

10. "We make a mistake," Harold Bloom writes in commenting on this passage, "if we read this as a projection of the child's conscience upon the external world. That he heard it is warrant enough for its reality" (Bloom, Introduction, 8). I find this remark opportune, since it so decidedly rejects the possibility of projection that seems to me obvious. (We may also note that it is not so much the child's "conscience" that is being projected as his predatory impulses, and in structural terms this projection marks a regression to more primitive forms of anxiety: there is a fear of retribution in the absence of a real threatening other, but that threat is still experienced as coming from without.) Bloom's insistence on the autonomous authority of the child's "enlarged senses" targets with precision the poetic and epistemologial crux of the passage. In doing so he seeks to abruptly resolve the unstable phenomenology of apprehension into a visionary source of authority. Yet the instability persists in his suggestively vague use of pronouns. What exactly is the "it" for whose reality the child's hearing is warrant? And for whom is that hearing by itself sufficient warrant? For the child? For the poet? For the reader? For whomever?

Four | The Autobiographical Object

1. The example is drawn from a psychoanalytic paper by R. Marcuszewicz with the interestingly equivocal title "Beitrag zum autistischen Denken bei Kindern" [A contribution to autistic thinking in children]. What Freud thus offers as a direct observation involves a series of citations.

2. I refer to Molly Anne Rothenberg and Joseph Valente's "Fashionable Theory and Fashion-able Women: Returning Fuss's Homospectatorial Look," a "critical response" to Fuss's essay "Fashion and the Homospectatorial Look," and to Fuss's counterresponse "Look Who's Talking, or If Looks Could Kill." Fuss's original essay appeared in 1992, but Rothenberg and Valente's response was not published until 1996, and thus after *Identification Papers* in 1995. Although Rothenberg and Valente do not refer to the latter, which probably was not yet available at the time they were writing their critique, one wonders whether the editors of *Critical Inquiry*, the publication venue for the entire exchange, were motivated to publish the response and counterresponse because of the interest generated by the recent appearance of the book.

3. The inscription of "the name of the father," not only in the name "du Peyrou" but in a whole series of key words in this passage (e.g., *pervenche, perdu, espère*), was pointed out to me by Jacques Derrida.

4. See, for example, his comments on "some of the flattest lines of which the English language is capable" in "Wordsworth and the Victorians" (*Rhetoric of Romanticism*, 87).

5. Cf. de Man's comment that the poem is an "epitaph written by the poet for him-

self, from a perspective that stems, so to speak, from beyond the grave. This temporal perspective is characteristic for all Wordsworth's poetry—even if it obliges us to imagine a tombstone large enough to hold the entire *Prelude* (*Romanticism and Contemporary Criticism*, 82).

Five | Action, Internalization, and Utterance

1. For a reading of the poem that closely parallels this one, see Jonathan Arac's discussion in *Critical Genealogies* (34–49), and in particular his conclusion that "rich beyond the wealth of kings through having textually achieved an impossible desire, the speaker has power to lay down the law to the 'dearest maiden'" (45).

2. One could argue that what I am advancing as a historical fact is an artifact of post-eighteenth-century canon formation and that in the literary culture from which Wordsworth emerged there were numerous women poets, publicly acclaimed as such. This is indisputable, but it also seems to me that the condition of this recognition was acquiescence to minority status. Emily Dickinson's "Divine Majority" refuses that acquiescence but also must spurn recognition.

3. The apostrophe to Dorothy at the end of "Tintern Abbey," while less evidently guilt ridden, also invokes the fiction of a generational difference between the poet and his sister in the interest of establishing an identification between Dorothy and William's youthful self. But the comparison with "Tintern Abbey" also calls attention to the epitaphic quality of the apostrophe in "Nutting" and the way Dorothy is invoked as the poet's legatee and successor. "These shades" denotes the place of the poem as haunted by the poet's memory, and the plea for tenderness bespeaks a sense of weakness and vulnerability. Wordsworth's exercise of male poetic authority, then, is crepuscular and anticipates a transmission and transformation of that authority that crosses gender boundaries.

Six | The Stewed Muse of Prose

1. In the fourth chapter of *A Room of One's Own*, Virginia Woolf speculates on the economic and social factors that led an emergent class of professional women writers to work almost exclusively in prose, even though, in her judgment, "The original impulse was to poetry" (69). If one contrasts this statement with Woolf's subsequent claim that "the whole structure . . . of the early nineteenth-century novel was raised, if one was a woman, by a mind which was slightly pulled from the straight, and made to alter its clear vision in deference to external authority" (77), the metaphysical underpinnings of the argument become clear. The drift of the chapter, however, is not toward a reclamation of "the original impulse" in its original form, but rather toward a revaluation of prose. For a critique of Woolf's views, see Patricia Yaeger's *Honey-Mad Women*, 181–84.

2. Cf. Geoffrey Hartman's claim in *Wordsworth's Poetry* that "the fates of the Old

Man and of the Solitary are mirror-images. . . .The vision which the Old Man may have had is experienced by the Solitary as he returns from the search for him" (309–10).

3. Cf. Hartman, *Wordsworth's Poetry*, 310.

4. My use of "end of the line" to articulate the relation between a more or less pictorial scene and the structure of narrative surrogacy it condenses is again borrowed from Neil Hertz. See especially the "Afterword" to *The End of the Line*.

5. Presumably the allusion is to Ezek. 40:39–43.

6. A more extended discussion of this passage would reinscribe the orienting function of the sacred within the economy of a conflict between the formal imperatives that organize the text and its representational claims. The exclamation, "I have been dead . . . / And now I live! Oh! Wherefore *do* I live?" whose chaotic symmetrics (one is reminded of the "violent harmonizing" of Wordsworth's verse that Hartman writes about in "The Poetics of Prophecy") compress an entire narrative of dying and returning from the dead, embodies this conflict at its most acute. But since all of *The Excursion*'s numerous instances of reported speech are given in an elevated iambic pentameter indistinguishable from the author's own voice, the threat of a comparable temporal confusion constitutes the very fabric of the work's language. (Thus Hazlitt's early complaint that "The recluse, the pastor, and the pedlar, are three persons in one poet" [*Complete Works*, 4:113] is ultimately a response to the way the uniform versification of *The Excursion* overrides, not only stylistically but logically, the grammatical and dramatic differentiation of speakers.)

7. As De Quincey was to explain in the 1856 revision of his *Confessions*. The passage is offered by Hayter in an appendix (214–15).

8. The critical apparatus of the Pléiade *Oeuvres complètes*, ed. Claude Pichois, provides a detailed account of the compositional history of both works.

9. In adherence to certain editorial principles, Pichois follows the tradition of printing "sacré bougre" as "s . . . b . . . ," although the manuscript offers no authority for the deletion. My text thus differs from Pichois's in this regard.

10. Thus, for example, in the notes to his critical edition of the *Petits Poèmes en prose*, Robert Kopp summarizes "La Soupe et les nuages" as follows: "Lost in contemplation of the 'marvelous constructions of the impalpable,' the narrator is brutally brought back to reality by his companion, who is perfectly oblivious to his elevation. Opposition of the ideal and the real" (340).

11. Although in contemporary French usage *bougre* is a fairly innocuous term, more or less equivalent to the British "bugger," in the nineteenth century the homosexual connotation was still strong enough for the word to be considered unprintable except by first initial. See, for example, the entry under *bougre* in volume 2 of Larousse's *Grande Dictionnaire universel du XIXe siècle* (Paris, 1866–79), which lists "sodomite" as its first definition. By contrast, the entry in the *Nouveau Larousse universel* (Paris, 1969) mentions no sexual connotation at all.

12. My description of the montage is based on Pichois's account in the editorial notes to "Les Yeux de Berthe" (Baudelaire, *Oeuvres complètes*, 1:1139–41). Pichois in-

cludes reproductions of parts of the montage, which is no longer intact, in his *Album Baudelaire* (220–22).

Seven | Drinking Rules!

1. The title of the current chapter invites a word of explanation and acknowledgment: a few Labor Days past while on vacation with my family in the Smokies, I was sitting at the edge of an indoor pool studying the "Pool Rules" posted on the wall ("No Running, No Jumping, No Diving, No Horseplay," etc.) while my daughter Carrie and her friend Sara, at the time both twelve, were changing in the locker room. All at once Sara, an avid swimmer, came barreling through the doors to the enclosure, cannonballed into the pool, and then, after a moment or two below the surface, surged up with her arms spread wide and exclaimed, "Water rules!" Two years later, in pondering my title for an MLA talk that was to evolve into this chapter, I recalled this happy conjunction.

2. See Estève, *Byron et le romantisme français,* especially chapter 7, "Le Déclin (1835–50)."

3. Caroline Defayis was born to an émigré family in London in 1793 and lived there until she was seven, when a Napoleonic decree of 1800 permitted her mother to return to France (her officer father having died in a 1795 counterrevolutionary expedition into Brittany) (Pichois, *Album Baudelaire,* 10–11).

4. In its immediate context, de Man's comment, which appears in the concluding paragraph of "Hegel on the Sublime," concerns specifically those of Baudelaire's prose poems that can be readily paired with particular poems in *Les Fleurs du mal,* but it clearly forms part of a more extended reflection linking art, the prosaic, and "a discourse of the slave." Since this chapter is in constant, if mostly mute, dialogue with that passage, I take this occasion to quote from it at greater length:

> The infrastructures of language, such as grammar and tropes, account for the occurrence of the poetic superstructures, such as genres, as the devices needed for their oppression. The relentless drive of the dialectic, in the *Aesthetics,* reveals the essentially prosaic nature of art; to the extent that art is aesthetic, it is also prosaic—as learning by rote is prosaic compared to the depth of recollection, as Aesop is prosaic compared to Homer, or as Hegel's sublime is prosaic compared to Longinus'. The prosaic, however, should not be understood in terms of an opposition between poetry and prose. When the novel, as in Lukács's interpretation of nineteenth-century realism, is conceived as an offspring, however distant or elegiac, of the epic, then it is anything but prosaic in Hegel's sense. Nor would Baudelaire's prose versions of some of the poems of *Les Fleurs du mal* be prosaic as compared to the metered and rhymed diction of the originals; all one could say is that they bring out the prosaic element that shaped the poems in the first place. Hegel summarizes his conception of the prosaic when he says: "It is in the slave that prose begins" (Im Sklaven fängt die Prosa an). Hegel's *Aesthetics,* an

essentially prosaic discourse on art, is a discourse of the slave because it is a discourse of the figure rather than of genre, of trope rather than of representation. As a result, it is also politically legitimate and effective as the undoer of usurped authority. (*Aesthetic Ideology*, 152–53)

5. That Byron plays with a vast range of styles is a staple of Don Juan criticism and is discussed extensively in McGann's *"Don Juan" in Context* (see especially chapter 5, "Style," and the appendix, "The Middle Style in 'Don Juan'"). Although McGann is clearly right to emphasize Byron's acute sensitivity to "the rhetorical rules of decorum" and "the theory of styles" (73), I doubt that his carnivalesque notion of "medley style" is adequate to differentiate the writing of *Don Juan* from, on the one hand, that Romantic poetry that Byron famously characterized as "the wrong revolutionary poetical system" and, on the other hand, the eighteenth-century precursors to whose poetic position he sought, in McGann's words, only a "partial return" (73). McGann's Byron preserves the multiple generic distinctions of his precursors while jettisoning the graduated hierarchical schema according to which they were organized in favor of a more encompassing idea of appropriateness. Thus "in the 'medley style' of Don Juan, there seems to be a time, and a style, for every purpose under heaven. Indeed, this more comprehensive ideal of appropriateness and propriety, in behavior and style alike, represents a fundamental ideal for life and poetry" (168). The question is whether one can forgo adherence to that larger, graduated, hierarchical schema without significantly impairing the generic and stylistic divisions whose relations it organizes. I cite the passage we are concerned with as evidence that one can't and that Byron doesn't, whether he will or no.

For a recent commentary on Byron's mixed style from the perspective of a working poet, see the late William Matthews's essay "Hail Muse, Etc." I quote the following passage from it in recollection of our talk about Byron and as particularly apposite to the concerns of this chapter: "The idea of a stew (or 'mess,' to look back to the Biblical meaning of 'mess of pottage,' which survives into our military diction: Mess Hall), with a little bit of everything in it, derives very exactly from Byron's rejection of the belle for the more inclusive range of effects and tones necessary to depict the daily emotional lives of mortals. The muse here is no glowing hologram, but kitchen help with gravy stains on her apron" (146). And, one might add, the mouth of a drill sergeant: see chapter 6 above, "The Stewed Muse of Prose."

6. As an instance of a comparable movement, consider the passage from *Twelfth Night* that appears as an epigraph (though on what authority is unclear) in many editions of *Don Juan:* "Dost thou think, because thou art virtuous, there shall be no more cakes and ale? Yes, by Saint Anne, and ginger shall be hot i' the mouth, too!"

7. For another recent discussion of this passage, see Mark Storey's *Byron and the Eye of Appetite*, 29–32.

8. James de Jongh has suggested to me that the figure also draws on a long-standing typological identification of the tree of life with the cross and pointed to the lyrics of "Strange Fruit" as a related instance of that identification.

9. Thus Christensen argues that "the distinction between power and strength" that is fundamental to his diagnosis of Byronism "reflects a fundamental difference between a commercialist code based on the depletion of substance and the acceleration of re-production and an aristocratic symbolic economy of expenditure" (*Lord Byron's Strength*, 5) and correlatively that "with Juan, in Juan, and through Juan, the Regency lord makes his uneasy peace with a postmodern ethic" (xxi).

10. Christensen makes a related claim when he argues that "the persistence of the pre-oedipal in the world of adults correlates with the persistence of a performative aris-tocracy in an age of gentrification" (*Lord Byron's Strength*, 17–18), though I would take issue with the implicit identification of "the pre-Oedipal" with "performative aristoc-racy."

11. Derrida remarks in passing on the "authoritarian" character of *Enivrez-vous* in *Donner le temps* (135). Needless to say, this book is influenced in ways too pervasive and contradictory to be specified by his work on the "strange" logic of supplementarity as that passes through the figure of the *pharmakos*.

12. As he does so evocatively and economically, for example, in the opening stanza of "L'Âme du vin":

Un soir l'âme du vin chantait dans les bouteilles:
Homme, vers toi je pousse, o cher désherité,
Sous ma prison de verre et mes cires vermeilles
Un chant plein de lumière et de fraternité!

[One evening the soul of wine sang in the bottles:
Man, toward you I send forth, O dear disowned one,
From beneath my glass prison and vermilion wax seals
A song full of light and of brotherhood.]

13. For a penetrating discussion of the paradoxical relation between time and "the law of the figure" in Baudelaire's prose poetry, see Barbara Johnson's brilliant analysis of "Le Galant Tireur" in "Disfiguring Poetic Language."

14. Baudelaire cites *Enrichissez-vous* as the watchword of its day in his 1851 appre-ciation of the socialist poet Pierre Dupont (*Oeuvres complètes*, 2:27). A few pages later in the same essay, following a passage based on Calderón whose cadences clearly an-ticipate the hypnotic lists of *Enivrez-vous*, as Jacques Crépet long ago noted (*Charles Baudelaire*, 324–25), he concludes, "Cette voix mystérieux chante d'une manière per-manente le remède universel" [This mysterious voice intones in a permanent manner the universal remedy] (*Oeuvres complètes*, 2:32).

Eight | "Le Bonheur Vomitif"

1. Thus placing him in paradoxical alliance with Rousseau. Indeed, the similarity of Baudelaire's concluding self-dramatization to the closing scene of the preamble to the *Confessions*, with its challenging avowals before an assembled multitude, is striking and illustrates how much Baudelaire's relation to an imagined public resembles Rous-

seau's. The singular and paradoxical role Rousseau plays in the argument of "Le Poème du hachisch" is discussed below.

2. In his recorded lectures on religious belief, Wittgenstein emphasized the incommensurability of religious expressions of belief or doubt with other differences of belief. "Suppose someone were a believer and said: 'I believe in a Last Judgement,' and I said: 'Well, I'm not so sure. Possibly.' You would say that there is an enormous gulf between us. If he said 'There is a German aeroplane overhead,' and I said 'Possibly I'm not so sure,' you'd say we were fairly near" (*Lectures,* 53). Following Stanley Cavell's reading of Wittgenstein and his insistence that the problem of skepticism cannot be exorcised by philosophy but is rather, to use one of Cavell's favored terms of analysis, "internal" to its experience, may we read Baudelaire's "satanism" as an incorporation—that is, as both an allegorical embodiment and an admission into the body of his own language and thought—of skepticism thus imagined? As the "incorporation" of what is radically unassimilable, the figuration disorganizes the opposition of inside and outside even as it deploys it. In the figure of "Satan as drug," the "inner" is the total field of representation secured by the opposition between inner and outer, while the "outer" is what disrupts this field—from "within" it.

3. It is clear, however, that these latter two identities are, to speak theologically, "attributes" of the former. In Baudelaire's initial enumeration, the three possibilities are coequal: "Je me figure un homme (dirai-je un brahmane, un poète ou un philosophe chrétien?)" [I picture a man (shall I say a Brahman, a poet, or a Christian philosopher?)], but subsequently Baudelaire refers to this figure simply as "le poète attristé," the saddened poet.

4. Thus when Marcel Ruff writes an introduction to a popular edition, he feels compelled to caution: "It is possible that the poetic beauty of the visions evoked by Baudelaire could arouse in certain readers a dangerous temptation should they remain unmoved by his purely spiritualist arguments" (24).

5. Baudelaire abruptly follows "Le Théâtre de Séraphin" with a dismissive gesture: "Il est temps de laisser de côté toute cette jonglerie et ces grandes marionettes" [It is time to set aside all this jugglery and these large marionettes] (*Oeuvres complètes,* 1:426). In the immediate context, it seems to be hashish that is the puppet master, but one could also, and in keeping with Saillet's suggestion, read the remark as a reference to Baudelaire's intricate textual manipulation of his narrative personae.

6. Baudelaire considered "Le Promeneur solitaire" as a possible title for his collection of prose poems. An allusion also occurs toward the end of the dedication to *Les Paradis artificiels:* "Tu verras dans ce tableau un promeneur sombre et solitaire, plongé dans le flot mouvant des multitudes" [You will see in this tableau a somber and solitary walker, one plunged in the moving flood of the multitudes] (*Oeuvres complètes,* 1:400). And this statement anticipates in turn the following sentence from the prose poem "Les Foules": "Le promeneur solitaire et pensif tire une singulière ivresse de cette universelle communion" [The solitary and pensive walker draws a singular intoxication from this universal communion] (*Oeuvres complètes,* 1:291). Finally, we may note

that the narrator of "Le Tir et le cimétière" refers to the focal subject of the text, and by extension of the collection, as "notre promeneur." For an extended reflection on the relation between a particular prose poem and a particular reverie, see Cynthia Chase's "Paragon, Parergon: Baudelaire Translates Rousseau" in *Decomposing Figures* (196–208).

7. That this question was very close to Baudelaire's mind in writing *Les Paradis artificiels* is clear from the following sentences in the dedication:

Est-il même bien nécessaire, pour le contentement de l'auteur, qu'un livre quelconque soit comprise, excepté de celui ou de celle pour qui il a été composé? Pour tout dire enfin, indispensable qu'il ait été écrit pour *quelqu'un*? J'ai, quant à moi, si peu de goût pour le monde vivant que, pareil à ces femmes sensibles et désoeuvrées qui envoient, dit-on, par la poste leurs confidences à des amis imaginaires, volontiers je n'écrirais que pour les morts.

Mais ce n'est pas à une morte que je dédie ce petit livre.

[Is it even really necessary, for the author's satisfaction, that any book whatever be understood, other than by him or her for whom it was written? Truth be told, indispensable that it be written for *someone*? As for myself, I have so little taste for the world of the living that, like those sensitive women with nothing to do who, it is said, post their confidences to imaginary friends, I would happily write for none but the dead.

But it is not to one dead that I dedicate this little book.] (*Oeuvres complètes*, 1:399–400)

8. Published posthumously, Baudelaire's collection of fifty prose poems (or fifty-one, if one includes the dedication to Houssaye) lacks a definitive title, with Baudelaire's editors alternating between *Petits Poëmes en prose* and *Le Spleen de Paris*, a vacillation that reflects the writer's own indecision (though Pichois makes a convincing case that in the very last years of his life Baudelaire had settled on the latter title [*Oeuvres complètes*, 1:1298–1300]).

9. The single most compelling piece of evidence in support of this claim is Baudelaire's prose poem "Le Thyrse," a text that has long been recognized as emblematizing the formal structure of the prose poetry and that is based on a paragraph from De Quincey's *Suspiria de Profundis* (where De Quincey uses the same figure to characterize the manner of his own prose). Furthermore, Baudelaire refers to both the thyrsus ("amalgame tout-puissant et indivisible du génie") [omnipotent and indivisible amalgam of genius] and his translation of De Quincey ("J'ai fait un tel amalgame que je ne saurais y reconnaître la part qui vient de moi" [I have made such an amalgam that I would be unable to recognize the share that comes from me]) (*Oeuvres completes*, 1:519) as "amalgams" defying analysis, a term that also figures centrally in his dedication to *Les Paradis artificiels* ("Le monde naturel pénètre dans le spirituel, lui sert de pâture, et concourt ainsi à opérer cet amalgame indéfinissable que nous nommons notre individualité" [The natural world penetrates the spiritual, provides its food, and thus concurs in the effecting of that indefinable amalgam that we call our individuality]) (1:399).

10. Jonathan Culler deals with this and several other of the passages I touch on in a rich article titled "Baudelaire's *Satanic Verses*," which appeared too recently for me to accord it here the attention it is due. Culler emphasizes the recurrent critical gesture by which we excise from our picture of a "modern" Baudelaire "the Baudelaire who invokes demons and the Devil" (86) and pointedly asks: "What threat does this figure pose that we need to set him aside?" (89).

11. A more detailed reading of this transformation would have to discuss at greater length the relation between sight and odor in Baudelaire. The specific phantasm in the passage at hand is the same as that latent in Derrida's description of the drug as an *épaisseur liquide*—identification of the drug with the human eye. The description of the drug as a "confiture verte, gros comme une noix, can be directly related to the motif of "green eyes" in Baudelaire, which appears in "Le Poison" as well as in several other pieces, including "La Soupe et les nuages," discussed in chapter 6, "The Stewed Muse of Prose."

Works Cited

Abrams, M. H. *Natural Supernaturalism: Tradition and Revolution in Romantic Literature.* New York: Norton, 1973.

———, ed. *The Norton Anthology of Literature.* New York: Norton, 1970.

Alighieri, Dante. "Letter to Can Grande Della Scala." In *Critical Theory since Plato,* ed. Hazard Adams, 121–23. New York: Harcourt Brace, 1971.

Arac, Jonathan. *Critical Geneaologies: Historical Situations for Postmodern Literary Studies.* New York: Columbia University Press, 1987.

Bateson, F. W. *Wordsworth: A Reinterpretation.* London: Longmans, 1965.

Baudelaire, Charles. *Correspondance.* Ed. Claude Pichois and Jean Ziegler. 2 vols. Paris: Gallimard, Bibliothèque de la Pléiade, 1973.

———. *Oeuvres complètes.* Ed. Claude Pichois. 2 vols. Paris: Gallimard, Bibliothèque de la Pléiade, 1975–76.

———. *Petits Poèmes en prose (Le Spleen de Paris).* Ed. Robert Kopp. Paris: Jose Corti, 1969.

———. *Petits Poëmes en prose.* Vol. 3 of *Oeuvres complètes de Charles Baudelaire.* Ed. Jacques Crépet. Paris: Louis Conard, 1926.

Benjamin, Walter. *Illuminationen: Ausgewählten Schriften.* Frankfurt am Main: Suhrkamp, 1969.

Bloom, Harold. "The Internalization of Quest-Romance." In *Romanticism and Consciousness: Essays in Criticism,* ed. Harold Bloom, 3–24. New York: W. W. Norton, 1970.

———. Introduction to *Wordsworth's "Prelude,"* ed. Harold Bloom. New York: Chelsea House, 1990.

Broglie, Gabriel de. *Guizot.* Paris: Perrin, 1990.

Butler, Judith. *Bodies That Matter.* New York: Routledge, 1996.

———. *Gender Trouble: Feminism and the Subversion of Identity.* New York: Routledge, 1990.

Butor, Michel. "Les Paradis artificiels." In *Essais sur les modernes,* 7–13. Paris: Gallimard, 1964.

Byron, George Gordon, Lord. *Don Juan.* Vol. 5 of *Lord Byron: The Complete Poetical Works.* Ed. Jerome J. McGann. 5 vols. Oxford: Clarendon Press, 1986.

Caruth, Cathy. "Past Recognition: Narrative Origins in Wordsworth and Freud." In *Empirical Truths and Critical Fictions: Locke, Wordsworth, Kant, Freud,* 43–57. Baltimore: Johns Hopkins University Press, 1991.

———. "'Unknown Causes': Poetic Effects." *Diacritics* 17, 4 (1997): 78–85.

Carver, Raymond. *What We Talk about When We Talk about Love: Stories.* New York: Vintage, 1989.

Cavell, Stanley. *Must We Mean What We Say?* New York: Scribner's, 1967.

———. *A Pitch of Philosophy: Autobiographical Exercises.* Cambridge: Harvard University Press, 1994.

———. *The World Viewed: Reflections on the Ontology of Film.* New York: Viking Press, 1971.

Chase, Cynthia. *Decomposing Figures: Rhetorical Readings in the Romantic Tradition.* Baltimore: Johns Hopkins University Press, 1986.

Christensen, Jerome. *Lord Byron's Strength: Romantic Writing and Commercial Society.* Baltimore: Johns Hopkins University Press, 1993.

Clarke, Colin. *Wordsworth.* Cambridge: Cambridge University Press, 1960.

Collings, David. *Wordsworthian Errancies: The Poetics of Cultural Dismemberment.* Baltimore: Johns Hopkins University Press, 1994.

Crépet, Eugene. *Charles Baudelaire.* Revised and completed by Jacques Crépet. Paris: Albert Messein, 1919.

Culler, Jonathan. "Baudelaire's *Satanic Verses.*" *Diacritics* 28, 3 (1998): 86–100.

de Man, Paul. *Aesthetic Ideology.* Ed. Andrzej Warminski. Minneapolis: University of Minnesota Press, 1996.

———. *Allegories of Reading.* New Haven: Yale University Press, 1979.

———. *Blindness and Insight: Essays in the Rhetoric of Contemporary Criticism.* 2d ed. Minneapolis: University of Minnesota Press, 1983.

———. *The Rhetoric of Romanticism.* New York: Columbia University Press, 1984.

———. *Romanticism and Contemporary Criticism: The Gauss Seminar and Other Papers.* Ed. E. S. Burt, Kevin Newmark, and Andrzej Warminski. Baltimore: Johns Hopkins University Press, 1993.

De Quincey, Thomas. *Confessions of an English Opium Eater.* Signet ed. Ed. Alethea Hayter. New York: New American Library, 1971.

Derrida, Jacques. *De la grammatologie.* Paris: Éditions de Minuit, 1967.

———. *Donner le temps.* Vol. 1. *La Fausse Monnaie.* Paris: Galilée, 1991.

———. "Fors." In *Cryptonomie: Le Verbier de l'homme aux loups,* 7–73. Paris: Aubier-Flammarion, 1976.

———. *Of Grammatology.* Trans. Gayatri Chakravorty Spivak. Baltimore: Johns Hopkins University Press, 1976.

———. "La Pharmacie de Platon." In *La Dissémination,* 69–197. Paris: Éditions de Seuil, 1972.

Estève, Edmond. *Byron et le romantisme français.* Geneva: Slatkine Reprints, 1973.

Evans, Margery. *Baudelaire and Intertextuality: Poetry at the Crossroads.* Oxford: Oxford University Press, 1993.

Ferguson, Frances. *Wordsworth: Language as Counter-Spirit.* New Haven: Yale University Press, 1977.

Freud, Sigmund. *The Standard Edition of the Complete Psychological Works of Sigmund Freud.* Ed. and trans. James Strachey. 24 vols. London: Hogarth Press, 1953–74.

Fuss, Diana. *Identification Papers.* New York: Routledge, 1995.

Gingrich, Newt. Interview by Ted Koppel. *Nightline.* ABC, WABC, New York, 2 April 1998.

Guiette, Robert. "Des 'Paradis artificiels' aux 'Petits poëmes en prose.'" In *Études Baudelairiennes*, 178–84. Paris: La Baconnière, 1973.

Hartman, Geoffrey. *The Unremarkable Wordsworth.* Minneapolis: University of Minnesota Press, 1987.

———. *Wordsworth's Poetry, 1787–1814.* New Haven: Yale University Press, 1971.

Haverkamp, Anselm. *Leaves of Mourning: Hölderlin's Late Work.* Trans. Vernon Chadwick. Albany: State University of New York Press, 1996.

Hazlitt, William. "Observations on Mr. Wordsworth's Poem *The Excursion.*" In *The Complete Works of William Hazlitt*, ed. P. P. Howe, vol. 4. London, 1930.

Hegel, G. W. F. *G. W. F. Hegel on Art, Religion, Philosophy: Introductory Lectures to the Realm of Absolute Spirit.* Ed. J. Glenn Grey. New York: Harper and Row, 1970.

Hertz, Neil. *The End of the Line.* New York: Columbia University Press, 1985.

———. "Lurid Figures." In *Reading de Man Reading*, ed. Wlad Godzich and Lindsay Waters, 82–104. Minneapolis: University of Minnesota Press, 1989.

———. "More Lurid Figures." *Diacritics* 20, 3 (1990): 2–27.

Hoeges, Dirk. *François Guizot und die französische Revolution.* Frankfurt am Main: Peter Lang, 1981.

Johnson, Barbara. *Défigurations du langage poétique.* Paris: Flammarion, 1979.

———. "Disfiguring Poetic Language." In *A World of Difference*, 100–115. Baltimore: Johns Hopkins University Press, 1987.

Kaplan, Edward K. *Baudelaire's Prose Poems: The Esthetic, the Ethical and the Religious in "The Parisian Prowler."* Athens: University of Georgia Press, 1990.

Keats, John. *Collected Poems.* Ed. Miriam Allott. London: Longmans, 1970.

Kelley, Theresa. *Wordsworth's Revisionary Aesthetics.* Cambridge: Cambridge University Press, 1988.

Kermode, Frank. *The Genesis of Secrecy.* Cambridge: Harvard University Press, 1979.

Klein, Melanie. "A Contribution to the Psychogenesis of Manic-Depressive States." In *Contributions to Psychoanalysis: 1921–1945*, 282–338. London: Hogarth Press, 1948.

Kneale, J. Douglas. *Monumental Writing: Aspects of Rhetoric in Wordsworth's Poetry.* Lincoln: University of Nebraska Press, 1988.

Knoepflmacher, Uri. "Genre and the Integration of Gender: From Wordsworth to George Eliot to Virginia Woolf." In *Victorian Literature and Society: Essays Presented to Richard D. Altick*, ed. James R. Kincaid and Albert J. Kuhn, 94–118. Columbus: Ohio State University Press, 1984.

Kristeva, Julia. *Pouvoirs de l'horreur.* Paris: Gallimard, 1978.

———. *Soleil noir: Dépression et melancholie.* Paris: Gallimard, 1987.

Lehrer, Ronald. *Nietzsche's Presence in Freud's Life and Thought: On the Origins of a Psychology of Dynamic Unconscious Functioning.* Albany: State University of New York Press, 1995.

Liu, Alan. *Wordsworth and the Sense of History.* New Haven: Yale University Press, 1987.

Lyu, Claire. "'High Poetics': Baudelaire's 'Le Poème du hachisch.'" *MLN* 109 (1994): 698–740.

Marx, Karl, and Frederick Engels. *The German Ideology.* Part 1. Ed. C. J. Arthur. New York: International Publishers, 1989.

Matthews, William. "'Hail Muse, Etc.'" In *Touchstones: American Poets on a Favorite Poem,* ed. Robert Pack and Jay Parini, 143–47. Hanover, N.H.: Middlebury College / University Press of New England, 1996.

Mayes, Elizabeth. "The Fantasy of Internalization in the Theoretical Imaginary." *Representations* 62 (spring 1998): 100–110.

McGann, Jerome J. *"Don Juan" in Context.* Chicago: University of Chicago Press, 1976.

Meissner, W. W. *Internalization in Psychoanalysis.* New York: International Universities Press, 1984.

———. "A Note on Internalization as Process." *Psychoanalytic Quarterly* 45 (1976): 374–93.

Montaigne, Michel Eyquem de. *Oeuvres complètes.* Ed. Maurice Rat. Paris: Gallimard, Bibliothèque de la Pléiade, 1962.

Nietzsche, Friedrich. *Ecce Homo.* Trans. Walter Kaufmann. New York: Vintage, 1969.

———. *On the Genealogy of Morals.* Trans. Walter Kaufmann and R. J. Hollingdale. New York: Vintage, 1969.

———. *Werke in drei Bände.* Ed. Karl Schlecta. Munich: Karl Fisher, 1966.

Onorato, Richard. *The Character of the Poet: Wordsworth in "The Prelude."* Princeton: Princeton University Press, 1971.

Palmer, R. R., ed. and trans. *From Jacobin to Liberal: Marc-Antoine Jullien, 1775–1848.* Princeton: Princeton University Press, 1993.

Parker, Reeve. *Coleridge's Meditative Art.* Ithaca: Cornell University Press, 1975.

Pichois, Claude, ed. *Album Baudelaire.* Paris: Gallimard, Bibliothèque de la Pléiade, 1974.

———. *Baudelaire.* Trans. Graham Robb. London: Hamish Hamilton, 1989.

———, comp. *Lettres à Charles Baudelaire.* Études Baudelairiennes. Paris: La Baconnière, 1973.

Pommier, Jean. *Dans les chemins de Baudelaire.* Paris: Jose Corti, 1945.

Poulet, George. *Studies in Human Time.* Trans. Elliott Coleman. New York: Harper Torchbooks, 1959.

Redfield, Marc, ed. "Addictions." Special issue of *Diacritics* 27, 3 (1997): 1–112.

Rosanvallon, Pierre. "Guizot et la question du suffrage universel au XIXe siècle." In *François Guizot et la culture de son temps,* ed. Marina Valensise, 129–45. Paris: Gallimard, Éditions de Seuil, 1991.

Rousseau, Jean-Jacques. *Oeuvres complètes*. Ed. Bernard Gagnebin and Marcel Raymond. Paris: Gallimard, Bibliothèque de la Pléiade, 1964.

———. *The Confessions*. Trans J. M. Cohen. Harmondsworth, U.K.: Penguin, 1982.

Ruff, Marcel, ed. *Les Paradis artificiels*. By Charles Baudelaire. 1860. Paris: Garnier-Flammarion, 1966.

Saillet, Maurice. "Baudelaire et l'épreuve des excitants." In *Sur la route de Narcisse*, 99–103. Paris: Mercure de France, 1958.

Schafer, Roy. *Aspects of Internalization*. New York: International Universities Press, 1968.

———. "Internalization: Process or Fantasy?" *Psychoanalytic Study of the Child* 27 (1972): 411–36.

———. *A New Language for Psychoanalysis*. New Haven: Yale University Press, 1976.

Schopenhauer, Arthur. *The World as Will and Representation*. Trans. E. F. J. Payne. New York: Dover, 1969.

Sedgwick, Eve Kosofsky. *The Epistemology of the Closet*. Berkeley: University of California Press, 1990.

———. "A Poem Is Being Written." In *Tendencies*. Durham: Duke University Press, 1993.

Shelley, Mary Wollstonecraft. *Frankenstein*. Ed. Maurice Hindle. New York: Penguin Books, 1986.

Sperry, Stuart M. "Tragic Irony: 'The Fall of Hyperion.'" In *Keats the Poet*, 310–35. Princeton: Princeton University Press, 1994.

Storey, Mark. *Byron and the Eye of Appetite*. New York: St. Martin's Press, 1986.

Tompkins, Silvan. *Shame and Its Sisters: A Silvan Tomkins Reader*. Ed. Eve Kosofsky Sedgwick and Adam Frank. Durham: Duke University Press, 1995.

Wittgenstein, Ludwig. *Lectures and Conversations on Aesthetics, Psychology, and Religious Belief*. Berkeley: University of California Press, 1967.

———. *Philosophical Investigations*. 3d ed. New York: Macmillan, 1958.

Woolf, Virginia. *A Room of One's Own*. London. 1957.

Wordsworth, Dorothy. *Journals*. Ed. Ernest de Sélincourt. 2 vols. London, 1951.

Wordsworth, William. *The Excursion*. Vol. 5 of *The Poetical Works of William Wordsworth*. Ed. Ernest de Sélincourt and Helen Darbishire. 5 vols. Oxford: Clarendon Press, 1958.

———. *The Prelude: 1799, 1805, 1850*. Ed. Jonathan Wordsworth. New York: W. W. Norton, 1979.

———. *The Prelude: A Parallel Text*. Ed. J. C. Maxwell. Harmondsworth, U.K.: Penguin Books, 1971.

———. *Selected Poems and Prefaces*. Ed. Jack Stillinger. Boston: Houghton Mifflin, 1965.

Yaeger, Patricia. *Honey-Mad Women: Emancipatory Strategies in Women's Writing*. New York: Columbia University Press, 1988.

Index

Library of Congress Cataloging-in-Publication Data

Wilner, Joshua.
  Feeding on infinity: readings in the romantic rhetoric of internalization / Joshua Wilner.
    p. cm.
  Includes bibliographical references and index.
  ISBN 0-8018-6324-4 (alk. paper)
    1. European literature—Male authors—History and criticism. 2. Psychoanalysis
and literature—Europe. 3. Male authors—Psychology. 4. Romanticism—Europe.
5. Internalization. 6. Infinity.   I. Title.

PN603 .W55 2000
809'.9145'019—dc21
                                                        99-049403